The Best 125 Meatless Italian Dishes

Susann Geiskopf-Hadler
Mindy Toomay

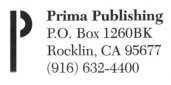

Prima Publishing
P.O. Box 1260BK
Rocklin, CA 95677
(916) 632-4400

Library of Congress Cataloging-in-Publication Data

Geiskopf-Hadler, Susann
    The best 125 meatless Italian dishes / Susann Geiskopf-Hadler, Mindy Toomay.
       p.   cm.
    Includes index.
    ISBN 1-55958-560-9
    1. Cookery, Italian 2. Vegetarian cookery. 3. Cookery (Pasta) I. Toomay, Mindy. II. Title. III. Title: Best one hundred twenty-five meatless Italian dishes.
    TX723.G35   1994
    641.5945—dc20   94-21791
                                        CIP

96 97 98 99 A A 10 9 8 7 6 5 4 3

Printed in the United States of America

How to Order:
Single copies may be ordered from Prima Publishing, P.O. Box 1260BK, Rocklin, CA 95677; telephone (916) 632-4400. Quantity discounts are also available. On your letterhead, include information concerning the intended use of the books and the number of books you wish to purchase.

We dedicate this book to that nameless cook who first ventured to combine olive oil and garlic with bread.

Acknowledgments

A special thanks, once again, to our friends at Prima Publishing for their continuing faith in this cookbook series. Thanks also to our loyal readers for adding this volume to their collections. We trust that these recipes will be enjoyed as much by your family and friends as they have been by ours.

From Susann, thanks to the vegetable vendors, the cooks—even the bus drivers—of Italy, for so passionately sharing their wonderful cuisine. Thanks, Dad, for that first trip and the wonderful meals and adventures we had there. A heartfelt thanks to Guy Hadler, Joseph Angello, and Gracie Caramanno for the multi-coursed feasts that continue to inspire, as well as satisfy.

From Mindy, thanks to Della and Dino Beltrami and their daughter Kathryn for making me welcome at their family table. Della's mastery in the kitchen awakened me to the delights of Italian home cooking. And thanks to Tad Toomay, who outdid himself as exhuberant cheerleader and recipe taster throughout the many months of testing and retesting.

Buon appetito!

Contents

Contents   *vii*

Almost Instant Recipes

The following list is a guide to the recipes in this book that require 30 minutes or less to prepare, from start to finish. This earns them our Almost Instant designation, which appears under the titles on the recipe pages. Pizzas are included on this list because one can find good-quality prepared pizza crusts or frozen bread dough for pizzas at the supermarket.

In addition, this book includes many other quick-to-prepare recipes not labeled Almost Instant because they call for precooked beans or require some time for baking or marinating. These are great do-ahead recipes.

Vegan Recipes

The vegan diet—which excludes meat, dairy products, and eggs—depends entirely on the nutrients found in the plant kingdom. We provide the following index of vegan recipes as a convenience for those who have embraced this approach to healthful eating. If you are interested in this dietary option, do your research, and pay close attention to food combining to ensure proper nutrition.

Vegan Recipes

Introduction

The foods of Italy are beloved the world over, cherished for their robust flavors and fresh ingredients. For centuries, Italian cooks have relied on olive oil, fresh herbs and vegetables, rice and cornmeal, and wheat in the form of hearty breads and pasta, as the staples of their sumptuous and diverse cuisine.

Italian cuisine is home cooking at its most simple and relaxed, to be savored with family and friends. Once you master the basics of Italian ingredients and techniques, this style of cooking quickly becomes second nature and allows for a great deal of adaptation and innovation.

Much Italian cuisine takes little time to prepare. Many of our recipes require no more than 30 minutes from start to finish. A list of these Almost Instant dishes appears on page x.

A few Italian classics—such as ravioli, gnocchi, and focaccia—are relatively time-intensive and may be intimidating to the novice. Once the procedures are understood, however, they become simple and familiar, and you'll look forward to preparing these dishes whenever time allows.

The cuisine of Italy is roughly divided between that of the northern regions and that of the south. In the north, dairy products such as butter and cheese have always been readily available and are prominent in traditional dishes. Another important distinction is that polenta and rice appear more frequently on Northern Italian tables than does pasta. In Southern Italy, on the other hand, pasta and savory breads have long been staples. Influenced by the warm Mediterranean climate, Southern Italian dishes feature sun-loving vegetables such as olives, tomatoes, eggplants, peppers, fennel, and basil.

In this book, we include our renditions of classic Northern and Southern Italian fare, as well as many wonderful *fantasias*, dishes based on an imaginative use of Italian ingredients rather than on tradition.

We encourage you to invite family and friends to the table to share one of the world's healthiest and best-loved cuisines.

Stocking
the Pantry

Since most Italians shop daily at the market rather than going to the supermarket once a week, their cuisine emphasizes fresh, seasonal ingredients. During spring, for instance, the market's best asparagus, fava beans, and artichokes would be preferred. Summer brings excellent vine-ripened tomatoes, peppers, and eggplants. During fall and winter, root vegetables such as potatoes and turnips play a prominent role, along with cool season crops like broccoli, cauliflower, and chard.

Such fresh ingredients are brought home and combined with the following staples, which no Italian kitchen would be without. In the United States, most of them are carried by major supermarkets and large metropolitan areas often have Italian grocery stores that carry fine imported items.

Beans

Dried beans are wonderfully nutritious, delicious, and economical, and have a place in all the cuisines of the world. In Italy, favorite types include cannellini beans (also known as white kidney beans), garbanzo beans (also known as chickpeas), cranberry beans, and lentils. Garbanzo beans and lentils are readily available in American supermarkets; cannellini and cranberry beans may require some looking in Italian specialty food stores. They are worth seeking out, however. Cooking instructions for dried beans are provided on page 30.

We also keep canned beans in our pantries for occasions when we don't have time for the rather lengthy soaking and cooking process required for dried beans. Select low-sodium or no-salt-added brands, and rinse canned beans before using to remove any undesirable additives that may affect the flavor. Canned beans can be mushy, so they work best in soups or stews, where a firm texture is less crucial than it would be in a salad, for instance.

The fava bean (also called broad bean) is another Italian favorite and is used both fresh and dried. Fresh favas in their large, coarse pods are available only for a brief time in late spring.

Cheeses

The Italians love cheeses, and have developed some of the world's most distinctive varieties. Their flavors are most pronounced when they are brought to room temperature before using.

The following cheeses are most common to Italian cooking.

Asiago The most notable of the cheeses of Venice, Asiago is enjoyed when fresh and soft in Italy, but is usually found aged and dried in the United States. We use it in a few of our recipes as a flavorful, dry grating cheese.

Fontina True Italian fontina is a cow's milk cheese from the Valle d'Aosta, in the Alpine region of Italy. Its flavor is delicate, buttery, almost nutty, and its creamy texture melts well.

Goat Cheese *Caprini* is the term encompassing all goat cheeses produced in Italy. In general, Italian goat cheese is crumbly in texture and piquant, even salty, in flavor. Since it is rarely available in the United States, any mild, crumbly, white goat cheese, or a crumbly sheep cheese like feta, can be used where our recipes call for goat cheese.

Gorgonzola This blue-veined cow's milk cheese is traditionally made in the Lombardy region. *Dolcelatte* gorgonzola is creamy, almost buttery, in texture. A more pungent, crumbly variety is also available. Either type may be used in our recipes.

Gruyère In Lombardy, near Italy's border with Switzerland, a cheese is made that is very similar to Swiss Gruyère. Called *groviera,* it is slightly sweet and characterized by large holes. Since *groviera* is rarely available in American markets, our recipes call for the Swiss version.

Mascarpone Mascarpone is a double-cream cheese coagulated with citric acid, which is responsible for its slightly sour flavor. High in butterfat with a thick, heavy consistency, it is used primarily in delicate pasta dishes and desserts.

Mozzarella Fresh Italian mozzarella is made from buffalo's milk and is purchased and eaten the same day it is made. The fresh mozzarella typically sold in the United States is made from cow's milk and packed for the market in its own whey.

It has a unique soft yet dense texture, and a slightly sweet blandness that combines well with many seasonings. Where our recipes call for fresh mozzarella, there is no substitute. Most American supermarkets sell a dry, firm mozzarella cheese, typically in the shape of a ball. This cheese bears little resemblance to fresh Italian mozzarella, but is a flavorful melting cheese. It is simply called "mozzarella," without the "fresh" designation, in our recipes.

Parmesan   The very best and only true Parmesan is *Parmigiano-Reggiano*. It is made by specially trained artisans from skimmed cow's milk, exclusively in the Emilia-Romagna region, where the city of Parma is located. Precise, centuries-old techniques are followed to produce the highly prized nutty, tangy, slightly salty cheese. Its texture is crumbly but not dry, and its color is straw yellow. It combines uniquely and deliciously with other ingredients and is the premier grating cheese of Italy. Buy it in small wedges, preferably cut directly from a large wheel, and grate it as needed. Never buy pregrated Parmesan, as it is dry and tastes sour.

Ricotta   Ricotta cheese is soft, unsalted, and grainy. It is made from the whey of cow's milk and is highly perishable, so it is seldom imported from Italy. The American-made version is different from that available in Italy, but perfectly acceptable. Whole-milk and part-skim varieties are available. Our recipes call for part-skim ricotta, which we find to be perfectly rich-tasting and delicious.

Romano   *Pecorino* is the Italian term that designates all sheep's milk cheese, and versions of pecorino are made in many regions of Italy. It is a sharp, salty cheese, typically aged and dried for grating. The most common pecorino sold in America is Romano (sometimes called Pecorino Romano). Its strong bite is characteristic of many Southern Italian dishes. Contrary to the assumption of many American cooks, Romano is not inter-changeable with Parmesan, as its flavor is far stronger.

Garlic and Onions

Needless to say, garlic is an absolute essential in Italian cooking. Its pungent punch defines many classic dishes. Fresh garlic is sold in bulbs, which should be firm when you squeeze them. Garlic is past its prime when it dries and shrivels in the paper skin or when it begins to show green sprouts at the top. Store garlic bulbs in a dry, airy spot.

The people of Italy are also quite fond of onions. They are used in raw form when a tangy crunch is desired; however, most often they are sautéed in olive oil or butter, which brings out their natural sugars and mellows their flavor. White, red, and yellow globe onions all have distinct flavors and textures. Select firm onions with no signs of sprouting. Store them in a cool, dry place.

Leeks, another member of the onion family, are particularly prized by Northern Italian cooks. They add a subtle onion note to dishes in which globe onions would overpower more delicate flavors. The best quality leeks are 1½ inches or less in diameter and have crisp, fresh-looking greens. Wrap them tightly in plastic and store them in the refrigerator. Typically, the green portion is trimmed away before cooking and can either be discarded or added to the stockpot.

Mushrooms

The white button mushrooms most common in American supermarkets are mild in flavor but quite delicious. In recent years, new cultivation techniques have made fresh "wild" mushrooms, with their distinctive earthy flavors, available to many

American markets. Some of our recipes call for the big, meaty portobello mushrooms. Chanterelles, morels, and criminis are other types that provide a robust flavor in certain dishes. We use them to enrich soups, sauces, and fillings—often in combination with standard button mushrooms.

The porcini mushroom is a highly prized wild mushroom frequently used, both fresh and dried, in Italian cuisine. The dried variety is readily available and will keep indefinitely. Dried porcini are reconstituted in hot water before using. The soaking liquid is extremely rich in flavor and is strained and used, never discarded.

Nuts

Italians love nuts and use them extensively in their cuisine. They are essential ingredients in many desserts, while some varieties—such as almonds, chestnuts, pine nuts, and walnuts—show up in savory dishes as well.

Pine nuts (*pignoli* in Italian) may be a new ingredient to many American cooks. They are the seeds harvested from the cones of the stone pine common to the Mediterranean regions of Italy. These small, oval nuts have a creamy color and texture and a unique rich flavor. They are often toasted to intensify the taste.

Shelled nuts should be stored in the refrigerator because their oils easily turn rancid and bitter.

Olive Oil and Butter

The premier cooking medium of Italian cuisine, olive oil appears regularly in this book. "Extra virgin" olive oil comes from the first pressing of the finest unripe olives. It delivers a powerful olive color, aroma, and flavor that is delicious in salads and in other raw preparations, such as pesto. "Virgin" olive oil is from slightly riper olives and has a higher level of acidity. It is suitable for many cooking uses, such as sautéing. "Pure" olive oil is the lowest grade, derived from the second or third pressing of the olives. Where the robustness of extra virgin olive oil is essential in our recipes, we have so specified. Elsewhere, we simply call for olive oil, and suggest you use the best quality you can afford. The taste of olive oil can vary greatly from brand to brand. Sample several small bottles before deciding which you prefer.

Some of our recipes, particularly those using classic Northern Italian ingredients, call for butter. Unsalted butter is always preferred for its sweet, creamy quality.

Pasta

Dried commercial pasta is generally made with hard durum-wheat flour (semolina) and without eggs. Dried semolina pasta has a sturdy texture and a distinctive taste that combines well with both delicate and robust sauces. Good pasta, when cooked al dente, is not rubbery, gummy, or starchy in the mouth. We keep many different shapes and sizes of dried semolina pasta in our pantries.

Today most markets carry a wide variety of excellent imported and domestic pasta products. We recommend you sample several brands until you find one you particularly like. Purchase dried pasta made from 100 percent durum-wheat semolina flour and water.

Fresh or homemade pasta is usually an egg and all-purpose flour preparation. It has a softer texture and is indispensable for stuffed pastas. When time doesn't permit making ravioli dough from scratch, however, you can take a shortcut and substitute fresh wonton wrappers, a widely available Chinese noodle.

Commercially prepared fresh noodles are now sold at many supermarkets. Their shelf life is extremely short, so look at the dates on the packages. Fresh pasta that sits too long at the market develops an off flavor that no sauce, however inspired, can mask. In most cases, dried semolina pasta will be a superior choice to the supermarket pasta that is labeled "fresh."

Polenta

Polenta is simply ground dried corn, known as cornmeal to most Americans. The Italians have a unique way of preparing it that has been a staple in certain Northern Italian regions for hundreds of years. Though non-Italians usually think of pasta as the national food of Italy, polenta and rice are more traditional in the north.

We keep both fine and coarse cornmeal in our pantries. Typically, soft polenta preparations are made from the fine variety, and the coarse variety is used in dishes where a firmer texture is desired, such as baked casseroles or grilled polenta dishes. Meal ground from either yellow or white corn is acceptable, though yellow polenta is much preferred in Italy.

Rice

Northern Italy is world-famous for the classic creamy rice preparation called risotto. Risotto requires a specific short, oval-shaped rice imported from Italy; the best-loved variety is Arborio.

In dishes where a creamy texture is not desired, we recommend regular long-grain white rice. Do not, however, substitute instant rice, as its texture and flavor are inferior.

Herbs and Spices

Fresh herbs are at the heart of some of Italy's most treasured dishes. Almost every Italian household keeps an herb garden, even if it's only a window box on a balcony, and we encourage you to do the same. Herbs are easy to grow and hardy. If you choose not to grow your own, look for fresh herbs in the produce section of major supermarkets or at vegetable stands.

Dried herbs and spices are readily available and have their uses, particularly in long-cooking soups or stews when you want all the flavors to combine into a unified whole. But keep in mind that dried herbs are not interchangeable for fresh in the recipes in this book.

The following are the most frequently used herbs and spices in Italian cooking.

Basil   The appetizing peppery aroma and flavor of fresh basil is unsurpassed in Italian cooking. Fresh basil is typically not cooked, but rather is added just before the dish is served.

Chili Flakes   Dried, crushed red chilies, including the seeds, are frequently used in the bold cooking of Southern Italy. Different brands or batches can vary in intensity. A good rule of thumb is to start with a very small amount and add more if a spicier dish is desired.

Fennel Seed   Fresh fennel is a popular vegetable in Italy. Its dried seeds will impart a licoricelike flavor to a dish. The seeds are usually crushed with a mortar and pestle before using.

Marjoram   Marjoram gives dishes a slightly sweet, floral flavor. Its delicacy will be lost if combined with strongly flavored herbs and spices.

Mint   Our recipes can be made with any of the common fresh mints, such as spearmint or peppermint.

Nutmeg   Nutmeg has a deliciously sweet, nutty flavor. When used with too heavy a hand, however, a bitterness develops that can overpower the dish. Our recipes call for freshly grated whole nutmeg. You may purchase a special nutmeg grinder or use the fine-holed side of a standard kitchen grater. Commercially ground nutmeg may be used, but is inferior in flavor.

Oregano   Fresh oregano is mild and aromatic. When dried, the flavor intensifies and can be quite strong. Both varieties have their uses in Italian cooking.

Parsley   Parsley is used in its fresh form, never dried. The curly leaf variety and the flat-leaf Italian variety are interchangeable in our recipes, though their raw texture is somewhat different. Italian cooks prefer the flat-leaf variety because it is slightly sweeter and more aromatic.

Rosemary   Rosemary is one of the most popular herbs in Italian cooking. Fresh rosemary is intensely aromatic and usually preferred. The dried herb, though not suitable for all uses, does have its place.

Saffron   The flavor of saffron in uniquely pungent, yet subtle. Saffron is essential to a few classic Italian dishes, for the golden yellow color it imparts as much as for its flavor. Saffron threads are the dried stamens of crocus flowers, harvested by hand, which explains the high price tag. However, a little goes a long way. We recommend buying saffron threads rather than powdered saffron.

Sage   This savory, woodsy herb is quite popular in Northern Italian cuisine. The herb is almost always used fresh. Dried sage leaves are occasionally used, but never the powdered form.

Capers

Capers are the unopened buds of a type of wild nasturtium common to certain regions of the Mediterranean. The buds are typically packed in vinegar, though they sometimes come packed in salt. Salted capers should be rinsed thoroughly before being used. Large capers (*capote*) and small capers (*nonpareil*) are interchangeable in our recipes, though very large ones may require mincing before being added to a dish.

Olives

Olive trees are a major feature of the Italian landscape, and the fruits have been used in Italian cooking for centuries. Green olives are the unripe fruit of the olive tree, while black olives have been left on the tree to ripen. The fruit must be cured to mellow its bitterness. Varieties are cured in salt, oil, or brine. Small, smooth, purplish black Gaeta olives and dry oil-cured black olives appear frequently in traditional Italian dishes. Our recipes call for the latter, which are more readily available in this country. The black olives canned in water, most common in American supermarkets, are not appropriate substitutes for the varieties called for in our recipes.

Stock

Freshly made stocks have real soul that canned and powdered broths can't imitate. We have provided simple instructions for making vegetable stock at home using ingredients you probably have on hand in your kitchen. Homemade stock can be refrigerated for several days or frozen for a longer period. In a pinch you may prepare stock from vegetable bouillon cubes, with different but acceptable results. Look for a low-sodium or no-salt-added brand.

Tomatoes

Pear-shaped tomatoes are preferred in Italian cooking because they have a firmer, meatier texture and less juice and seeds than round salad tomatoes. For optimum flavor, enjoy fresh tomato dishes only when vine-ripened tomatoes are available at the markets. At other times, good quality canned tomatoes are a better choice for cooked dishes than fresh. Look for brands that contain no additives.

Imported Italian tomato paste sold in a tube is convenient to use when only a tablespoon or two is called for in a recipe. It is dependably sweet and rich.

Italian cooks often recommend dried tomatoes packed in oil. Where our recipes call for dried tomatoes, however, we use plump dried tomatoes packed loose in cellophane bags or ones that we've dried ourselves. They are easily reconstituted in water and deliver intense tomato flavor without added oil.

Vinegar

Good wine vinegar begins with good wine, so don't immediately reach for the cheapest wine vinegar on your grocer's shelf. Sample different types and you'll discover the brands you most enjoy. Choice wine vinegars should appear clear, not cloudy, and should have a rich color.

In addition to white and red wine vinegars, we keep balsamic vinegar on hand. An invention of the Italian province of Modena, it is uniquely rich, dense, and mellow. True balsamic vinegar is made according to ancient techniques and aged ten to fifty years in wooden barrels before bottling. It is indispensable to certain Italian dishes.

Uncommon Vegetables

There are a few vegetables favored by Italian cooks that are available in American markets but unfamiliar to most American cooks.

Broccoli Rabe   Broccoli rabe is a wild form of the commercial broccoli to which Americans are accustomed. Known as *cime di rapa* or *rapini* in Italy, and sometimes sold as broccoli rape in American markets, this vegetable is prized for its sharp bitterness. It resembles a very thin, leafy broccoli stalk with no pronounced head. Most Italian markets and many local produce stands carry it from fall through early spring.

Cardoons   Cardoons are related to artichokes, although cardoon plants do not produce edible thistle flowers. The green leaves are trimmed from the stalks, and the stalks are peeled and cooked. When cooked, they are similar in flavor and texture to artichoke bottoms. Cardoons grow wild in parts of California, as they do in Italy. They are often available in Italian markets, and are easily cultivated in warm climates.

Escarole   A member of the chicory family, escarole has a tangy, almost bitter flavor. It tastes much like curly endive, but the leaves are darker green and have smooth edges.

Select escarole heads that have crisp, fresh-looking leaves with unblemished white bases. For raw use, discard the tough outer leaves, or save them to use in a cooked dish.

Fava Beans   Fava beans, also called broad beans, have a distinctive, succulent flavor. Part of the culinary crop is eaten fresh and the remainder is dried.

Fresh favas can be eaten either cooked or raw, although some people have difficulty digesting them raw. The large pods—ranging from six to twelve inches in length—host a bean that has a flavor unique among shell beans. Getting to them is an easy but time-consuming task. First the bean is removed from the pod, then it is blanched and peeled. Favas harvested while very young and tender may be eaten without peeling.

Select pods that are deep green and glossy, with well-developed, bulging seeds. Blackening at the pods' ends is a sign that the beans will not be of good quality. Pods will feel spongy, but should appear juicy and fresh. Favas in their pods will stay fresh for a few days if refrigerated in a plastic bag.

Fennel Fresh fennel looks similar to celery, with numerous stalks attached at their bases in overlapping layers to form a thick bulb. Its foliage, however, is feathery and the bulb is paler in color and more enlarged than that of a bunch of celery. Fennel has a pronounced licorice flavor that is unusual and delicious raw, mellowing to a delectable sweetness when cooked. Though the leaves and stalks are edible, it is the bulb portion that is sliced and used as a vegetable in Italian cooking.

In the markets, fennel is sometimes labeled with its Italian name, *finocchio*, or sweet anise. Look for fennel bulbs that have straight stalks protruding from a plump, tightly closed, white base. Wrap fennel in plastic and store it in the vegetable crisper, where the bulb will stay fresh for a few days.

Radicchio A member of the chicory family, radicchio adds a unique, mildly bitter accent to salads and other dishes. Though different colors are cultivated, the most common variety in American markets is mottled purple and white.

Shop for small, crisp leaves forming a loose, cabbagelike head. The color should be robust and glossy, with no brown spots. Wilted, tired-looking heads are too old. Wrap radicchio loosely in a plastic bag and store it in the refrigerator crisper. Wash the leaves and spin them dry just before using.

Wines and Spirits

It is no secret that Italians love wine, for drinking as well as cooking. Italy produces vast quantities of wine. Much of it is consumed by Italians, but a great deal is exported.

For cooking purposes, select a good wine, one that you enjoy drinking. The finished dish will be only as good as the sum of its ingredients—this is as true of wine as it is of any other component of a successful dish.

We select wines from California as well as from Italy for both cooking and drinking. We keep dry red and white varieties on hand, plus a few specialty wines for their unique flavors. Dry Marsala—imported from Sicily—dry sherry, and port appear in a few recipes in this book. Again, purchase the best quality you can afford.

Nutrition Alert

People who are concerned about nutrition base their food selection on factors beyond the outmoded "five basic food groups" concept. In 1992, the U.S. Department of Agriculture released the Food Guide Pyramid, presenting the food groups with new emphases. At the base of the pyramid are the foods from which we should get most of our calories. At the tip are the foods that should supply us with the fewest calories. (For a brochure depicting the Food Guide Pyramid and discussing the concept in detail, order Home and Garden Bulletin #252 from USDA, Human Nutrition Information Service, 6505 Belcrest Road, Hyattsville, MD 20782.)

The basic message of the pyramid is that we should cut down on fats and added sugars, as well as eat a variety of foods from the different groups. Our chief eating goals, says the USDA, should be variety, moderation, and balance. It is the overall picture that counts—what you eat over a period of days is more important than what you eat in a single meal. A diet primarily comprised of grains and cereal products (6–11 servings per day), vegetables (3–5 servings per day), and fruits (2–4 servings per day), combined with lowfat protein sources (2–3 servings per day) and lowfat dairy products (2–3 servings per day) conforms to the Food Guide Pyramid, creating a well-balanced mix of proteins, carbohydrates, and fats.

To some people, three to five servings of vegetables will sound like a lot, but serving sizes specified by the Food Guide Pyramid are moderate. A cup of leafy raw vegetables (as in a salad), ½ cup of cooked or chopped raw vegetables, ¾ cup of vegetable juice, or ¼ cup of dried fruit equals one serving. There is no need to measure—the servings sizes are only a guideline. Furthermore, a single dish may supply servings in more than one category: for example, a sandwich may provide a grain serving (the bread), a dairy serving (the lowfat cheese), and a vegetable serving (the lettuce, sprouts, and tomato).

The nutritional experts who designed the Food Guide Pyramid recommend eating a variety of vegetables to ensure getting all the nutritional benefits this vast family of foods can provide. They also recommend that at least one serving each day be high in vitamin A; at least one each day is high in vitamin C; at least one each day is high in fiber; and that we eat cruciferous vegetables several times each week.

Vitamins A and C are particularly important because they function in the body as antioxidants. Antioxidants are a class of nutrients that neutralize free radicals, unstable oxygen molecules that cause cell damage over time, increasing the body's vulnerability to serious disease. Vitamin A is present in animal products but can also be manufactured as needed by the body from the beta carotene in vegetables that are dark green (e.g., leafy greens and broccoli) or orange-yellow (e.g., sweet potatoes). Some quantity of vitamin C is present in most fruits and vegetables; the best sources include citrus fruits, strawberries, tomatoes, broccoli, leafy greens, and sweet potatoes.

Studies have shown that antioxidants help protect us against the development of heart disease and cancer, and may even slow the aging process. Cruciferous vegetables contain considerable quantities of antioxidants, as well as beneficial nitrogen compounds called indoles, which have been shown in recent studies to be effective cancer preventers.

The surgeon general and the American Heart Association are proponents of a semivegetarian approach to eating, which is based primarily on grains, vegetables, and fruits. The Food Guide Pyramid and other expert recommendations support semivegetarianism as an important aspect of a healthy lifestyle. The major shift required for many Americans is to view meat, if it is consumed at all, as a side dish or condiment.

Many studies are being conducted to determine optimal levels of various food components in the human diet. Our intent here is to provide an introduction to basic nutrition. For further investigation, check with your local librarian or bookseller for comprehensive reference works.

The recipes in this book have been analyzed for calories, protein, carbohydrates, fat, cholesterol, sodium, dietary fiber, and crude fiber. We discuss below the importance of each of these components.

Calories   It is important to be aware of your total caloric intake in a day, but more important is to note the source of the calories. Calories come from three primary sources: proteins, carbohydrates, and fats. Fats contain a greater concentration of calories than do carbohydrates or protein, and they are much harder for the body to metabolize. The U.S. Food and Drug Administration therefore suggests that the average American diet should be adjusted so that fewer calories come from fatty foods and more from carbohydrates. They specifically recommend that no more than 30 percent of the calories in our overall diets be derived from fat.

Fat Our bodies need some fat, as it is an essential component in energy production, but it is estimated that most of us consume six to eight times more fat than we need. High-fat diets are implicated not only in heart disease, but also in the development of some cancers, most notably of the colon and breast. Learning the basics about dietary fat is likely to contribute to a healthier—perhaps even longer—life.

There are nine calories in a gram of fat. A gram of protein or carbohydrate contains only four calories. Hence the less fat one consumes, the lower one's intake of calories and the lower one's percentage of calories from fat. Moreover, calories derived from dietary fats are more troublesome than calories from any other source, as the body is most efficient at converting fat calories into body fat.

Consider that the average tablespoon of oil contains fourteen grams of fat and 120 calories, while almost no fat is contained in a half cup of steamed brown rice (206 calories) or a cup of cooked broccoli (44 calories). This illustrates the volume of food that can be eaten without increasing one's fat-to-calories ratio.

Another way of monitoring fat intake is by counting fat grams consumed. The nutritional analysis provided with each of our recipes facilitates this by listing fat in total grams per serving. An easy way to calculate how much fat you should consume is to divide your body weight in half. This number is an estimate of the maximum fat in grams a moderately active person of your weight should ingest over the course of a day to maintain that weight.

Fats are divided into three categories: monounsaturated, polyunsaturated, and saturated. Saturation refers to the number of hydrogen atoms present in the fat, with saturated fats containing the most.

The primary reason to pay attention to the saturation level of fats is that diets high in saturated fats increase levels of blood cholesterol in some people—a risk factor in heart disease. Not only do monounsaturated and polyunsaturated fats not harm our hearts, they actually appear to help reduce cholesterol levels in the blood when eaten in moderation as part of an overall low-fat diet.

Therefore, it is wise to choose foods higher in polyunsaturated or monounsaturated fats than in saturated fats. To make this determination, remember that most saturated fats are of animal origin and are hard at room temperature (such as butter and cheese) and most unsaturated fats are of vegetable origin and are liquid at room temperature (such as olive and canola oils).

Nutritional research has suggested another positive aspect of consuming olive oil. In recent studies, it has been shown to lower the level of LDL cholesterol, which is instrumental in depositing fat on artery walls. At the same time, the artery-protecting benefits of HDL remain intact. Perhaps this begins to explain the relatively low rates of heart disease in Mediterranean countries.

Fiber   Dietary fiber—also called roughage—is material from plant foods that cannot be completely digested by humans. It provides the bulk necessary to keep the digestive and eliminative systems functioning properly. Foods high in fiber also tend to be high in beta carotene, low in fat, and filling enough to reduce our dependence on higher-fat foods.

In recent years, evidence demonstrating that dietary fiber promotes human health has mounted. Studies have linked high fiber intake with reduced risk of constipation; diverticulosis; colon, rectal, and breast cancer; heart disease; diabetes; and obesity. Because high-fiber diets tend to be low in fat and high in other health-promoting substances, it is difficult to prove fiber's individual protective effects. However, the connection is compelling and studies are ongoing.

Many doctors now recommend adding fiber to the diet. Even such slow-to-change organizations as the U.S. Department of Agriculture and the National Cancer Institute have recently made increased fiber consumption part of their standard recommendations for a healthy diet.

NCI recommends that we eat between 20 and 30 grams of fiber daily, but that our consumption not exceed 35 grams per day. Experts estimate that most Americans now eat only about half of that amount. A recent national food survey showed that diets including five servings of fruits and vegetables daily—as recommended in the Food Guide Pyramid—provide about 17 grams of fiber. When whole grains and legumes are included in the daily diet, it's easy to reach the recommended level.

Experts agree that fiber should come from foods, not supplements, which provide no nutrients. Ways to consume more fiber—along with valuable vitamins, minerals, and amino acids—include choosing whole grain rather than refined-flour products, not peeling fruits and vegetables, and eating dried peas and beans.

It is especially important for people on high-fiber diets to drink plenty of water, or the fiber can slow down or block healthy bowel functioning. Eating a great deal of fiber can cause gastrointestinal distress in people unaccustomed to it, so fiber content should be increased gradually.

The term "dietary fiber" encompasses both soluble and insoluble types. The dietary fiber value in our nutritional analyses includes both types; the crude fiber value refers to insoluble fiber only.

Protein   Since our bodies store only small amounts of protein, it needs to be replenished on a daily basis. However, though protein is needed for growth and tissue repair, it is not needed in abundance. The National Academy of Science's Food and Nutrition Board recommends 45 grams of protein per day for the average 120-pound woman and 55 grams for the average 154-pound man.

Some nutritionists think this is more protein than people usually need. Recent nutritional studies suggest, in fact, that the detrimental effects of excessive protein consumption should be of greater concern to most Americans than the threat of protein deficiency. While this debate continues, it makes sense to choose protein sources that are low in fat and, thus, calories.

Most people associate protein consumption with eating meat; however, the protein in our recipes derives from combining grains with legumes and from dairy products, and is quite sufficient to meet the body's protein needs.

Carbohydrates There is a common misconception that carbohydrates such as pasta, grains, and potatoes are high in calories and low in nutritive value. But starchy complex carbohydrates do not present a calorie problem; the problem is typically with the fats that are added to them.

Nutritional experts now suggest that more of our daily calories come from carbohydrates than from fats or protein, since the body draws energy more economically from carbohydrates. Carbohydrates are quickly converted into glucose, the body's main fuel.

Complex carbohydrates are low in fat and a good source of fiber. They should comprise a large share of our daily calories.

Cholesterol Numerous volumes have been written on cholesterol in recent years, and much is being discovered about its role in overall health and nutrition. Cholesterol is essential for the construction of cell walls, the transmission of nerve impulses, and the synthesis of important hormones. It plays a vital role in the proper functioning of the body and poses no problem when present in the correct amount. Excess cholesterol, however, is a major risk factor in the development of heart disease. The U.S. Senate Select Committee on Nutrition and Human Needs recommends that the average person consume no more than 300 milligrams of cholesterol per day. The best course of action is to have one's cholesterol level checked by a doctor, and follow his or her specific guidelines.

Recent studies have shown that the total amount of fat a person eats—especially saturated fat—may have more effect on the cholesterol level in the body than the actual cholesterol count found in food. Current evidence suggests that a high-fiber diet that's low in overall fat can reduce cholesterol levels, particularly the harmful LDL type. Vegetables are certainly major players in such a diet.

Sodium   The American Heart Association recommends that sodium intake be limited to 3,000 milligrams per day (a teaspoon of salt contains 2,200 milligrams of sodium). However, the actual physiological requirement is only about 220 milligrams a day. Sodium is essential for good health, since each cell of the body must be bathed continually in a saline solution. Yet high sodium intake disrupts this balance and is associated with high blood pressure and such life-threatening conditions as heart and kidney disease and strokes.

Many foods naturally contain some sodium, so you do not need to add much when cooking to achieve good flavor. Particularly if you have salt-related health concerns, dishes that taste a little bland unsalted can be seasoned with herbs or other salt-free alternatives. When our recipes call for salt, you may add less than the recommended amount, or none at all, if your doctor has drastically reduced your sodium intake.

Monitoring your intake of all these food components is important; however, unless you're under doctor's instructions, you needn't be overly rigid. It is preferable to balance your intake over the course of a day, or even several days, rather than attempting to make each meal fit the pattern recommended by nutritional experts. This approach allows you to enjoy a recipe that may be higher in fat or salt, for instance, than you would normally choose, knowing that at your next meal you can eliminate that component altogether to achieve a healthful daily balance.

The information given here is not set in stone; the science of nutrition is constantly evolving. The analyses for our recipes are provided for people on normal diets who want to plan wholesome meals. If your physician has prescribed a special diet, check with a registered dietician to see how these recipes fit into your guidelines.

We encourage you to spend some time learning about how foods break down and are used by the body as fuel. A basic understanding of the process and application of a few simple rules can contribute to a longer and—more important—healthier life.

Seven Simple Guidelines for a Healthy Diet
(from National Cancer Institute, U.S. Department of Health and Human Services)

1. Eat a variety of foods.
2. Maintain a desirable weight.
3. Avoid too much fat, saturated fat, and cholesterol.
4. Eat foods with adequate starch and fiber.
5. Avoid excessive sugar.
6. Avoid excessive sodium.
7. If you drink alcoholic beverages, do so in moderation.

An Introduction
to the Recipes

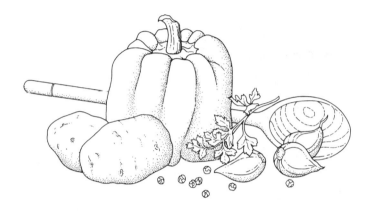

Traditional Italian cooks take their inspiration from whatever is in season and fresh at the market. At heart, Italian cooking is casual and earthy. It is an art, not a science, and relies on the best quality ingredients prepared simply and with gusto.

In each chapter's introduction, we have provided information to familiarize you with the various categories of Italian food. Please read these introductions for a comprehensive overview. But don't be dominated by rules. In the true spirit of Italian cooking, allow your enthusiasm and creativity free rein in the kitchen.

You will notice that our recipes list ingredients in an unconventional format, with the name of a food in the first column and the quantity required in a separate column to the right. This facilitates quick perusal of the ingredients, so you can determine whether you're in the mood for that particular dish or whether you have the required items on hand. We find this format particularly easy to follow, and hope you will agree.

Tips for Successful Cooking from Recipes

Follow the suggestions below to ensure a smooth and enjoyable cooking experience when working from written recipes.

- Use only the freshest, finest ingredients. Your finished dish will be only as good as the individual components that go into it, so don't compromise on quality.

- Read a recipe all the way through before beginning to cook. This will allow you to take care of any preliminary steps, such as bringing ingredients to room temperature, and will give you a solid grasp of the entire process.

- Set out your ingredients and equipment on the work surface before you begin. This will save you walking from one end of the kitchen to the other to rummage in a cupboard for the long-lost nutmeg, for instance, while neglecting whatever is cooking on the stove.

- For certain ingredients, quantities are by nature approximations. When we call for a large carrot, for example, the one you use may be more or less large than the one we used. This is nothing to worry about. When using a specific amount is essential to the success of a dish, we have provided cup or pound measurements. Otherwise, exercise your own judgment about which carrot in the bin is "large." Garlic amounts in our recipes refer to medium-size cloves. If you are using elephant garlic, or the tiny cloves at the center of a garlic bulb, adjust the number of cloves accordingly.

- Seasonings are a matter of personal taste. We have provided recipes for dishes that taste good to us, seasoned as we like them. Other people will prefer more or less of certain seasonings, such as salt or garlic.

- Serve hot food on warmed serving dishes and warmed individual plates so the food stays at optimal temperature as long as possible. This is easily accomplished by placing the dishes near the heat source as you cook; or warm your oven shortly before dinnertime, turn off the heat, and place the dishes there until needed.

Techniques for the Basics

Here we explain some basic techniques used in various recipes in this book. They are simple, quick procedures. Once you have mastered them, you will find them quite useful.

Blanching Vegetables

To blanch fresh tomatoes, drop them into boiling water. Within a minute or two, their skins will begin to split and pull away from the flesh. Remove the tomatoes with a slotted spoon to a bowl of cold water. When cool enough to handle, peel off the skins and cut out the stems.

A recipe will sometimes call for seeding the tomatoes after blanching. When cooled, cut the peeled tomatoes in half crosswise and gently squeeze to remove the juicy seed pockets.

Some recipes call for blanching other vegetables (also called parboiling) to cook them slightly before they are combined with other components of the dish. The purpose of blanching, in these cases, is to brighten the color and soften the texture. Wash the vegetables. Boil several cups of water in a large, lidded pot. When the water boils, drop in the vegetables. Blanching time will vary, usually from about two to five minutes, depending on the size and density of the vegetable. Check a piece for doneness from time to time; it should still be quite firm, but not as crunchy as its raw counterpart. When done, cool immediately in cold water, and drain.

Roasting Vegetables

Certain vegetables develop a delightful smoky flavor when roasted. Peppers lend themselves most readily to this type of preparation; tomatoes and small eggplants are other good candidates for roasting. Place the vegetables, whole or cut, under a very hot broiler and turn every few minutes until the surface is well charred and mostly black. Remove to a paper or plastic bag, fold to close, and set aside. The steam in the bag will finish the cooking process and the vegetables will become quite soft. When cooled, remove them from the bag and peel off the charred skin. Remove stems and/or seeds and proceed with the recipe. Alternately, you may char the vegetables on a hot coal or gas grill (see next technique).

Cooking on a Grill

In regions where summer brings high temperatures, outdoor grilling is a great alternative to stove-top cooking, which can heat up not only the kitchen but the entire house. In California, the climate allow us to enjoy grilled foods practically year-round.

To preheat a coal grill, start the charcoal at least 15 to 20 minutes before cooking begins so the proper temperature can be achieved in time. The grill is ready when the coals are glowing bright red and coated with a fairly thick layer of gray ash. Preheat a gas grill for at least 10 minutes or according to the manufacturer's specific directions.

Some safety tips: Set up the grill in an open area away from the house, and never attempt to move a hot grill. Do not cook on a charcoal fire in high winds. Avoid wearing flowing garments when cooking on a grill. Never squirt charcoal lighter fluid directly into a fire. Use long-handled utensils, and wear heavy-duty mitts. Make sure ashes are completely cold before discarding.

Reconstituting Dried Fruits and Vegetables

To get the most flavor from fruits and vegetables that have been dried, and to soften them to a chewable consistency, reconstitute before using.

The technique for fruits is to immerse them in warm water, fruit juice, brandy, or wine, and allow them to sit at room temperature until softened. The amount of time will vary from fruit to fruit. Do not let fruits sit any longer than necessary in the liquid, as their flavor and color will leach out.

For tomatoes, each degree of dryness—from papery to leathery to plump—calls for a slightly different technique. Paper-dry or leathery ones should be covered with boiling water and allowed to plump 15 to 30 minutes. The goal is a chewable, but not mushy, texture. Drain well, reserving the liquid, if desired, for use in a soup or sauce, and chop or mince the tomatoes as the recipe instructs. Depending on how chewy they are, the plumper type may not need reconstituting.

Reconstitute all varieties of dried mushrooms by soaking them for 30 minutes or so in warm water. Usually, the recipe will suggest straining and saving the soaking water to use where liquid is needed in the dish. Check the reconstituted mushrooms for grit and rinse well, if necessary.

Another option is to cover dried fruits or vegetables with water in a small bowl and heat them in a microwave oven for a minute or two, or until soft.

Baking Garlic

Preheat the oven or toaster oven to 350 degrees F. Rub off as much papery skin as possible from the garlic bulb, but do not break it up into individual cloves. Slice about ½ inch off the pointed end of the bulb, rub the cut surface evenly with ⅛ teaspoon of olive oil, and place in a covered clay or glass dish (or wrap the bulbs in foil). Bake for 45 minutes to an hour. Garlic is done when the bulb feels very soft when gently squeezed. Take the roasted garlic out of the oven and allow it to cool.

Remove the garlic from its skin by squeezing the cloves from the bottom. The garlic will slide out of the cut end as a soft paste. Patiently remove any bits of skin that cling to the garlic paste, and proceed with the recipe. Whole baked garlic bulbs may also be served as a delicious spread for bread or crackers.

Cooking Beans

The texture and flavor of freshly cooked dried beans are far superior to those of canned varieties, and dried beans are economical. Where our recipes call for cooked beans, we strongly recommend you use freshly cooked ones. As a general rule of thumb, 1 cup of dried beans will yield 2–2½ cups of cooked beans.

Before cooking beans, rinse them thoroughly to remove surface dirt and sort them carefully. Often small dirt clods, pebbles, or other foreign objects will find their way through the factory sorters and into the market bean bins. Also discard beans that are shriveled or discolored.

We usually soak dried beans for several hours before cooking. This softens them slightly and shortens the cooking time. Cover with plenty of fresh water and leave at room temperature overnight, loosely covered with a tea towel or lid. A quicker method is to cover them with boiling water and leave them to soak, loosely covered, for a few hours. Drain off the starchy soaking liquid.

Cover the beans with fresh water and boil until tender. Depending on the type of bean and its age, this can take from 30 minutes to 2 hours. Test frequently so as not to overcook. For most uses, beans should be boiled until they yield easily to the bite, but are not mushy. If they are to be cooked further after boiling, as in a casserole, take them from the pot when barely al dente.

You may wish to add garlic, bay leaves, and/or chili flakes to the cooking water, but wait to salt the pot until the beans are tender and ready for their final seasoning, because cooking in salt can give beans a tough or rubbery texture.

Beans freeze well. Cook them in larger quantities than a recipe calls for, then freeze the surplus beans in their cooking liquid in small, measured portions.

Toasting Seeds and Nuts

Place a single layer of nuts or seeds in a cast-iron skillet over medium-high heat on the stove. Shake the pan frequently. Soon the nuts or seeds will be golden brown, emitting a wonderful roasted aroma. Remove immediately from the pan and set aside until needed.

Frequently Used
Homemade Ingredients

When our recipes call for such ingredients as vegetable stock or bread crumbs, you may purchase commercial varieties. For top quality and economy, however, make your own. It's easier than you think to keep homemade "convenience" foods on hand.

Bread Crumbs and Cubes

If you have part of a whole grain or thick-crusted loaf that has dried out, simply break the bread into chunks and chop it in a food processor to either coarse or fine consistency. It is sometimes useful to have seasoned bread crumbs on hand, made by mixing dried herbs and granulated garlic into the crumbs before storing.

You can also prepare dried bread crumbs from fresh bread. Preheat the oven to 350 degrees F. Use your hands to crumble the bread onto a dry baking sheet. Place in the oven for 15 minutes, then turn off the heat, and allow crumbs to continue drying for about half an hour.

When recipes call for bread cubes, simply cut fresh or slightly stale bread into the desired size and bake as just described. For seasoned bread cubes (croutons), see the following recipe.

Dried bread crumbs and cubes will keep for long periods in a dry place in an airtight container.

Seasoned Croutons

ALMOST INSTANT, VEGAN

In flavor and texture, these far surpass the expensive boxed croutons you find on the supermarket shelf. They are utterly simple to prepare, and store well at room temperature in a glass jar with a tight-fitting lid.

Yield: 8 cups

Fresh or stale thick-crusted bread, cubed	**8**	**cups (about ½ pound)**
Extra virgin olive oil	**¼**	**cup**
Garlic	**3**	**cloves, minced**
Dried oregano	**½**	**teaspoon**
Dried marjoram	**½**	**teaspoon**

Preheat the oven to 450 degrees F. Cut the bread into ¾-inch cubes. Place the olive oil in a small bowl and whisk in the garlic. Rub the dried herbs between the palms of your hands to finely crush them and add to the oil, whisking to combine. Arrange the bread cubes on a cookie sheet. Use a pastry brush to lightly coat every side with the oil. Place in the oven and bake for 10 minutes, tossing them after about 5 minutes, until the croutons are golden brown. Remove from the oven and cool before using. Store in an airtight container for up to a week, or freeze for up to 3 months.

Each ¼ cup provides:

71	Calories	7 g	Carbohydrate
1 g	Protein	81 mg	Sodium
4 g	Fat	0 mg	Cholesterol
0 g	Dietary Fiber		

Italian Vegetable Stock

VEGAN

Any vegetable trimmings can be included in the stockpot. This recipe emphasizes Italian seasonings and vegetables commonly used in Italian cooking, but virtually any combination of vegetables, including fresh or dried mushrooms and herbs, will make a good stock. Don't feel compelled to measure precisely; just use about twice as much water as mixed vegetables, by volume, and don't allow a single vegetable to predominate.

Yield: about 10 cups

Water	14	cups
Russet potatoes, not peeled	2	medium, diced
Yellow onions	2	medium, diced
Green bell pepper	1	medium, diced
Celery	1	rib, chopped
Mushrooms	½	pound
Assorted vegetables, chopped (see note on page 35)	2	cups
Garlic	6	cloves, chopped
Bay leaves	2	
Dried rosemary	2	teaspoons
Dried basil	2	teaspoons
Dried thyme	½	teaspoon
Peppercorns	½	teaspoon
Salt	¾	teaspoon

Put the water on to boil in a large stockpot over medium-high heat. Add all the vegetables, herbs, peppercorns, and salt, and bring to a boil. Reduce heat to low and simmer, uncovered, 45 minutes. Turn off the heat and allow to steep for an additional 15–30 minutes before straining into glass jars. Any stock you do not use immediately may be stored for several days in the refrigerator or for several months in the freezer.

Note: Good choices for the assorted vegetables would be fresh fennel bulb, broccoli stalks, spinach or chard stems, and carrots. If you include broccoli or other members of the cabbage family, keep the total quantity of these at no more than 1 cup, as the flavors and aromas of such strong vegetables can dominate the stock.

Each cup provides:

23	Calories	5 g	Carbohydrate
0 g	Protein	182 mg	Sodium
0 g	Fat	0 mg	Cholesterol
0 g	Dietary Fiber		

Crostini

ALMOST INSTANT, VEGAN

Crostini are nothing more than oven-baked slices of toast, but they must be made with an excellent fresh bread. They can be served with any number of tasty toppings; we provide two recipes in the "Anti-pasti and Salads" chapter. Crostini can be made several hours or a day ahead of time, and kept at room temperature in a loosely closed cloth or paper bag.

Yield: about 12 servings

Fresh thick-crusted bread   1   1-pound loaf

Preheat the broiler, or preheat a coal or gas grill, to medium (page 29). If the bread has a long, skinny shape (such as a baguette) cut it across the width into ½-inch slices. If you are using a dome-shaped loaf, cut it in half, then cut each half into ½-inch slices. Arrange the slices in a single layer on the broiler pan or directly on the grill. Cook about 2 minutes per side until the bread is lightly browned and crisp on the outside, but still soft and chewy on the inside. Don't bake the bread too long, or it will dry out completely.

Each serving provides:

108	Calories	19 g	Carbohydrate
3 g	Protein	219 mg	Sodium
1 g	Fat	0 mg	Cholesterol
1 g	Dietary Fiber		

An Introduction to the Recipes

Antipasti and Salads

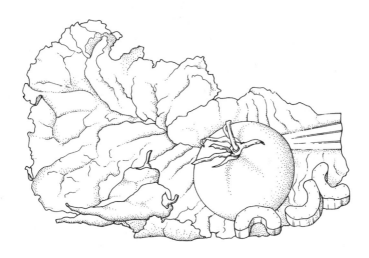

At a classic Italian meal, a combination of succulent dishes is offered before the first course as an appetite teaser. These dishes are called *antipasti* in recognition of their place at the beginning of the meal, before more substantial courses are served. Italian antipasti are comparable to what Americans call appetizers.

On the other hand, a green salad that might precede or accompany an American main dish would typically follow the main course in Italy, to refresh the palate. Such a salad is often simply a variety of fresh, crisp greens tossed with fruity olive oil, wine vinegar or lemon juice, salt, and pepper. Other cooked or raw vegetables are sometimes added for variety. The final four recipes in this chapter are suitable for serving after the main course of a formal meal.

Enjoy the other recipes as traditional antipasti, presented individually or in whatever combination you wish. Serving larger portions, you can make a complete meal of a diverse selection of antipasto dishes. When planning an antipasto platter, you could also include frittate, focaccia, or any savory dish that tastes good at room temperature.

The more substantial dishes in this chapter can stand alone as light suppers or lunch entrées, as indeed they sometimes do in Italy.

Tips and Tools

- Take the time to wash salad greens carefully, since dirt and sand are frequently lodged among the leaves. Be sure to dry greens so the water that clings to them doesn't dilute the dressing.
- Marinated vegetables or beans should be prepared well in advance so the flavors can blend and balance before serving.
- We prefer leafy green salads chilled, but toss just before serving with room-temperature dressing. All the other dishes in this chapter are most flavorful when served at room temperature. Recipes will indicate when a dish should be refrigerated, but always set it out for 30 minutes to an hour before serving.
- Bread is commonly served with antipasti, not to be buttered and eaten alone, but rather to help scoop vegetables onto the fork and to sop up all the delicious juices on the plate.

Olives Marinated with Parsley and Garlic

VEGAN

Antipasti presentations in Italy often include olives. We offer this particular marinated olive to guests as an appetite teaser, along with more substantial antipasti. The dry oil-cured black olives called for here have a wrinkled appearance. Most Italian markets carry these olives in their delicatessen case or in jars imported from Italy. Leftover marinated olives may be stored in a jar in the refrigerator for several weeks. Bring them to room temperature before serving for maximum flavor. It is hard to estimate the serving size for this recipe since we usually serve these olives as part of the antipasti platter or with focaccia.

Yield: 32 antipasto servings

Extra virgin olive oil	⅓	**cup**
Fresh-squeezed lemon juice	⅓	**cup**
Fresh Italian parsley, minced	¼	**cup**
Garlic	6	**cloves, minced**
Dry oil-cured black olives, unpitted	2	**pounds**

Whisk the oil, lemon juice, parsley, and garlic together in a small bowl. Add the olives and toss to coat. Allow to marinate at room temperature for several hours before serving. Toss every so often so that the marinade coats all of the olives.

Each serving provides:

118	Calories	3 g	Carbohydrate
1 g	Protein	930 mg	Sodium
12 g	Fat	0 mg	Cholesterol
1 g	Dietary Fiber		

Grilled Italian Garlic Bread

ALMOST INSTANT, VEGAN

Known in Italy as bruschetta, *this simple and scrumptious snack is the original Italian garlic bread. In the classic version, the bread is grilled over a hot fire to give it the characteristic marks. A perfectly good version, however, can be made by broiling the bread. The toasted bread is then brushed with plenty of good fruity olive oil and fresh minced garlic. You may use any long baguette or dome-shaped loaf with a thick crust and coarse texture.*

Yield: 12 antipasto or side-dish servings

Extra virgin olive oil	6	**tablespoons**
Garlic	4	**cloves, minced**
Fresh thick-crusted bread	1	**1-pound loaf**

Preheat a coal or gas grill to medium (page 29). Combine the oil and garlic in a small bowl and set aside.

If the bread has a long, skinny shape (such as a baguette) cut it across the width into ½-inch slices. If you are using a dome-shaped loaf, cut it in half, then cut each half into ½-inch slices. Arrange the slices in a single layer directly on the grill.

Cook about 2 minutes per side until the bread is lightly browned and crisp on the outside, but still soft and chewy on the inside. Don't dry out the bread by grilling too long. Remove from the grill and brush one side liberally with the oil and garlic. Serve immediately.

Each serving provides:

169	Calories	20 g	Carbohydrate
3 g	Protein	220 mg	Sodium
8 g	Fat	0 mg	Cholesterol
1 g	Dietary Fiber		

Crostini with Topping of Tomatoes, Fresh Basil, Garlic, and Capers

VEGAN, ALMOST INSTANT

The crostini—toasted bread slices—and the tomato topping can both be made hours ahead of serving time. This dish works well as an antipasto or as the salad course of any Italian-inspired summer feast. However, we often make a light meal of it, with the addition of fresh mozzarella cheese and a fruity Italian red wine. There is one cardinal rule: You must use vine-ripened, round salad tomatoes and basil leaves that are fresh from the plant. You may adjust the amount of garlic to your liking—several large cloves would not be too much for a garlic lover.

Yield: 12 side-dish servings

Crostini	1	**1-pound loaf**
Tomatoes	1½	**pounds (3 medium)**
Fresh basil leaves	1	**cup, firmly packed**
Garlic	3	**cloves, minced**
Capers, drained	2	**tablespoons**
Extra virgin olive oil	2	**tablespoons**
Fresh-squeezed lemon juice	2	**teaspoons**
Salt	¼	**teaspoon**
Pepper		**Several grinds**

Prepare the crostini according to the directions on page 36.

Cut the tomatoes in half crosswise and squeeze out the seed pockets. Cut out the stems and discard them. Dice the tomatoes uniformly. Wash and dry the basil leaves and sliver them with a sharp knife. Toss with the tomatoes in a bowl. Add the garlic, capers, olive oil, lemon juice, salt, and pepper, and stir to combine well. Set aside at room temperature for up to a few hours.

Put the tomato mixture in a shallow serving dish and place the crostini alongside in a basket. Diners serve themselves, mounding the topping onto single slices of bread.

Each serving provides:

146	Calories	23 g	Carbohydrate
4 g	Protein	303 mg	Sodium
4 g	Fat	0 mg	Cholesterol
2 g	Dietary Fiber		

Crostini with Dried Tomato and Olive Pesto

VEGAN

Rich and pungent, a little of this spread goes a long way. Though the crunch of crostini is satisfying, you could skip the toasting step and simply serve the pesto with sliced country bread. A favorite cheese may be served alongside. This spread will keep up to several days in a closed container in the refrigerator. In fact, it improves with age. Leftover crostini can be saved in an airtight jar at room temperature for a day or two.

Yield: 12 antipasto servings

Crostini	1	**1-pound loaf**
Dried tomatoes, reconstituted (see page 29)	½	**cup**
Dry oil-cured black olives, pitted	½	**cup**
Fresh Italian parsley leaves	⅓	**cup**
Extra virgin olive oil	3	**tablespoons**
Garlic	2	**cloves, chopped**
Fresh-squeezed lemon juice	2	**teaspoons**
Dried oregano	1	**teaspoon**
Dried red chili flakes	½	**teaspoon**
Salt		**A scant pinch**

Prepare the crostini according to the directions on page 36.

Combine all remaining ingredients in a food processor and puree to a thick paste consistency. This may be done well ahead of time. Keep at room temperature for several hours, or in the refrigerator for up to several days, but return to room temperature before serving.

Serve the pesto in a pretty bowl or crock with a small knife or paddle for spreading.

Each serving provides:

162	Calories	21 g	Carbohydrate
4 g	Protein	440 mg	Sodium
7 g	Fat	0 mg	Cholesterol
1 g	Dietary Fiber		

Seasoned Olive Oil

ALMOST INSTANT, VEGAN

This variation of the classic pinzimonio *makes enough dipping sauce for a party! We enjoy it with good crusty bread and/or raw vegetable pieces. Any leftover sauce can be stored in a jar and will keep for several weeks.*

Yield: 18 antipasto servings

The dipping sauce

Extra virgin olive oil	½	cup
Balsamic vinegar	2	tablespoons
Garlic	2	cloves, minced
Dried oregano	1	teaspoon
Dried basil	1	teaspoon
Dried red chili flakes	¼	teaspoon
Salt	⅛	teaspoon
Pepper		Several grinds

The dipping materials

Fennel bulb, including stalks	1	pound (1 medium)
Red bell pepper	½	pound (1 large)
Fresh thick-crusted bread	1	1-pound loaf

Place the oil in a shallow bowl. Whisk in the vinegar and garlic. Finely crush the oregano, basil, and chili flakes, then add to the oil mixture, along with the salt and pepper. Whisk together and allow to stand at room temperature for about 1 hour before serving.

Meanwhile, trim off the stalks of the fennel and slice the bulb in half lengthwise. Cut out and discard the small center core. Cut the fennel crosswise into ½-inch slices. Remove and discard the stem, seeds, and membranes of the pepper, and cut it into thin strips. Arrange the vegetables on a platter. Slice the bread and place it in a basket.

Serve the seasoned oil in a shallow bowl alongside the vegetables and bread.

Each serving provides:

138	Calories	16 g	Carbohydrate
3 g	Protein	173 mg	Sodium
7 g	Fat	0 mg	Cholesterol
1 g	Dietary Fiber		

Marinated Garbanzo Beans with Onion, Pepperoncini, and Fontina

This wonderful antipasto uses pickled Italian pepperoncini. Super-markets often carry both Greek and Italian varieties. The Italian ones are less tart, and we prefer them in this dish. Serve on small plates, one per diner. Crostini, baguette slices, or crisp crackers would be a fine accompaniment, as would a bowl of olives. For a variation, use another type of Italian cheese, or none at all.

Yield: 8 antipasto servings

Italian pepperoncini, drained	½	**cup**
Cooked garbanzo beans*	2	**cups**
Red onion	½	**medium**
Fontina cheese	2	**ounces**
Red wine vinegar	¼	**cup**
Extra virgin olive oil	2	**tablespoons**
Salt		**A pinch**
Pepper		**Several grinds**
Italian parsley leaves, minced	¼	**cup**

Remove pepperoncini one at a time from the jar, gently squeezing their juice back into the jar. Put them in a measuring cup, stems attached, until you have ½ cup of firmly packed peppers. Place in a large bowl along with the beans. Cut the onion half lengthwise into ¼-inch slices. Separate the onion layers and

*Cook 1 cup of presoaked dried beans for 45 minutes to an hour (see page 30) until they are al dente. Alternatively, you may use canned beans, rinsed and well drained.

add to the bowl, along with the cheese. Toss to combine. Add 2 tablespoons pepperoncini brine, the vinegar, oil, salt, and pepper, and toss until well distributed. Add the parsley and toss again. Set aside at room temperature to marinate for up to several hours before serving. You may also refrigerate the dish for a day or longer, but return the beans to room temperature before serving.

Each serving provides:

133	Calories	13 g	Carbohydrate
6 g	Protein	157 mg	Sodium
7 g	Fat	8 mg	Cholesterol
2 g	Dietary Fiber		

Cannellini Beans
in Mint Marinade

VEGAN

The mint is a delightful, fresh surprise in this marinade. On the island of Sicily and in Southern Italy, fresh mint is used as a primary herbal seasoning. These beans are a wonderful antipasto by themselves or a tasty addition to an antipasti platter. You might also enjoy them served on butter lettuce leaves as a side dish.

Yield: 10 antipasto servings

Cooked cannellini beans *	**3½ cups**
Extra virgin olive oil	**⅓ cup**
Fresh-squeezed lemon juice	**¼ cup**
Salt	**¼ teaspoon**
Pepper	**Several grinds**
Fresh mint leaves, minced	**¼ cup**

Whisk together the oil, lemon juice, salt, and pepper in a medium-size bowl. Stir in the mint. Drain the cooked beans well and add them to the marinade. Gently toss to coat, then allow

*Cook 1½ cups of presoaked dried beans for 30–45 minutes (see page 30) until they are al dente. Alternatively, you may use canned beans, rinsed and well drained.

Antipasti and Salads

them to marinate at room temperature for several hours before serving. Any leftovers may be refrigerated but should be returned to room temperature before serving.

Each serving provides:

152	Calories	16 g	Carbohydrate
6 g	Protein	48 mg	Sodium
7 g	Fat	0 mg	Cholesterol
3 g	Dietary Fiber		

Fresh Fava Beans in Watercress Marinade

VEGAN

During spring and early summer, look for fresh fava beans in an Italian grocery or at a local farmers market. Fresh fava beans evoke a passion among Italians in America and Italy; there is no substitute for this large, tender bean. Prepare this dish as an annual early-spring indulgence—the flavor is worth the effort. The time-consuming part is preparing the beans; the rest of the dish is quick and easy. Three pounds of fresh beans yield about ¾ pound of shucked and peeled beans.

Yield: 8 antipasto servings

Fresh fava beans, in the pod	3	**pounds**
Extra virgin olive oil	¼	**cup**
Fresh-squeezed lemon juice	3	**tablespoons**
Garlic	1	**clove, minced**
Salt	¼	**teaspoon**
Pepper		**Several grinds**
Fresh watercress leaves, minced	¼	**cup**

Shell the beans, discarding the pods. Blanch the beans for 1 minute according to the directions on page 27, then cool them slightly and peel. Reheat the blanching water to a boil and add the beans. Cook them for just 2 minutes, until barely tender. Be careful not to overcook them. Drain the beans in a colander and rinse with cold water. Transfer them to a shallow bowl.

Whisk together the olive oil, lemon juice, garlic, salt, and pepper. Pour over the beans, then add the watercress and toss to combine. Allow to marinate at room temperature for about an hour before serving. This dish may be kept overnight in the refrigerator, but bring to room temperature before serving.

Each serving provides:

100	Calories	7 g	Carbohydrate
3 g	Protein	69 mg	Sodium
7 g	Fat	0 mg	Cholesterol
2 g	Dietary Fiber		

Grilled Peppers with Balsamic Vinaigrette

ALMOST INSTANT, VEGAN

We prefer to use several different colors of sweet peppers for this dish. The subtle difference in flavors is pleasing, and the colors make a pretty presentation. Serve it with a good crusty bread to sop up the extra dressing.

Yield: 6 side-dish servings

Extra virgin olive oil	3	**tablespoons**
Balsamic vinegar	1	**tablespoon**
Fresh-squeezed lemon juice	1	**tablespoon**
Garlic	1	**clove, minced**
Fresh basil leaves, minced	1	**tablespoon**
Fresh mint leaves, minced	1	**tablespoon**
Salt	⅛	**teaspoon**
Pepper		**Several grinds**
Sweet peppers	2	**pounds (4 large)**

Preheat a coal or gas grill to medium (see page 29). Whisk together the olive oil, vinegar, and lemon juice. Add the garlic, basil, mint, salt, and pepper. Whisk again and set aside.

Cut the peppers in half, discard the stems, seeds, and pithy membranes, then slice each half in thirds lengthwise. Place on a rack on the grill, cover the grill, and cook 12–15 minutes, turning several times during this time. They will char slightly and become limp. Arrange on a serving platter and pour the dressing over them. Serve immediately, or allow to marinate at room temperature for as much as several hours. They may also be covered and refrigerated for up to 2 days.

Each serving provides:

100	Calories	10 g	Carbohydrate
1 g	Protein	47 mg	Sodium
7 g	Fat	0 mg	Cholesterol
2 g	Dietary Fiber		

Sweet Peppers, Onions, and Tomatoes

VEGAN

Any color of bell peppers may be used. We particularly like a mix of red, yellow, and green ones. This antipasto can be made year-round using canned tomatoes if good fresh ones are not available. Variations of this dish appear in many restaurants throughout Southern Italy, served with crusty bread.

Yield: 8 antipasto servings

Fresh pear tomatoes	**1**	**pound**
Bell peppers	**2**	**pounds**
		(4 large)
Yellow onions	**2**	**medium**
Olive oil	**2**	**tablespoons**
Dried basil	**1**	**tablespoon**
Salt	**¼**	**teaspoon**
Pepper		**Several grinds**
Dry oil-cured black olives,		
pitted and chopped	**⅓**	**cup**
Capers, minced	**2**	**tablespoons**

Blanch and peel the tomatoes (see page 27), then chop them coarsely. Set aside. Remove and discard the stems, seeds, and pithy membranes. Cut the peppers lengthwise into ½-inch strips. Set aside.

Halve the onions lengthwise and cut the halves into thin slices. Heat the oil over medium heat in a large skillet and add the onions. Sauté until they are limp but not brown, about 5 minutes, stirring frequently. Add the tomatoes, basil, salt, and pepper. Reduce heat to low and cook about 5 minutes. Stir in the peppers. Cover and simmer about 15 minutes, until the peppers are tender. Remove from the heat and allow to sit in the pan, covered, for an additional 15 minutes. Transfer the mixture to a serving bowl and stir in the olives and capers. Allow to cool, then serve at room temperature or chilled.

Each serving provides:

119	Calories	16 g	Carbohydrate
2 g	Protein	309 mg	Sodium
6 g	Fat	0 mg	Cholesterol
4 g	Dietary Fiber		

Pickled Eggplant with Raisins and Sweet Red Peppers

VEGAN

This is a good dish to start in the morning so the eggplant has plenty of time to marinate. It is easy to finish and serve as an antipasto for the evening meal. These familiar ingredients are paired in a typically Southern Italian way. We use fresh red bell peppers that are roasted and peeled; however, you may substitute 1 cup of commercially prepared fire-roasted peppers if you wish.

Yield: 8 antipasto servings

Eggplant	1½	**pounds (1 large)**
White wine vinegar	½	**cup**
Fresh mint leaves, minced	2	**tablespoons**
Fresh oregano leaves, minced	1	**tablespoon**
Fresh basil leaves, minced	1	**tablespoon**
Garlic	2	**cloves, minced**
Salt	1	**teaspoon**
Pepper		**Several grinds**
Red bell peppers	1	**pound (2 large)**
Golden raisins	⅓	**cup**
Extra virgin olive oil	¼	**cup**

In a large saucepan, bring a couple of quarts of water to a boil. Trim the stem end from the eggplant, then cut it into ¾-inch cubes. Place the cubes in the boiling water and cook for 5 minutes over medium heat, until just fork-tender. Drain well and place in a shallow bowl.

Meanwhile, whisk together the vinegar, mint, oregano, basil, garlic, salt, and pepper. Pour this over the cooked eggplant and marinate in the refrigerator for 5–6 hours.

Roast the peppers according to the directions on page 29. Chop coarsely and set aside. Place the raisins in a bowl, cover with hot water, and allow them to sit for about 15 minutes to plump, then drain them well. Add the bell peppers, raisins, and oil to the eggplant. Toss to combine. Allow flavors to blend at room temperature for about 1 hour before serving.

Each serving provides:

114	Calories	14 g	Carbohydrate
2 g	Protein	270 mg	Sodium
7 g	Fat	0 mg	Cholesterol
2 g	Dietary Fiber		

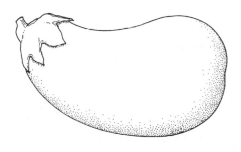

Caponata

VEGAN

*Versions of this famous dish have been made for centuries in Sicily.
All of the main ingredients are native to the area and abundant during the hot summer months. We like to serve it with colorful greens,
cheese, and bruschetta or crostini. This recipe makes a lot, so store
the leftovers in the refrigerator and enjoy them over the next few
days.*

Yield: 12 side-dish servings

Eggplant	3	pounds (2 large)
Salt	1	tablespoon
Pear tomatoes (or 1 14.5-ounce can)	1½	pounds
Extra virgin olive oil	¼	cup
Yellow onion	1	medium, chopped
Celery	2	ribs, chopped
Garlic	2	cloves, minced
Dried red chili flakes	¼	teaspoon
Green olives, water packed	1	7¾-ounce can (drained wt.)
Capers	2	tablespoons
Fresh Italian parsley, minced	¼	cup
Fresh-squeezed lemon juice	¼	cup

Trim off and discard the stem end from the eggplant. Cut the
eggplant into ¾-inch cubes. Place the cubes in a colander
and sprinkle with salt. Set aside in the sink or over a bowl and
allow to drain for 1 hour. Rinse briefly and dry thoroughly with
paper towels.

Meanwhile, blanch and peel the tomatoes according to the directions on page 27. Chop them into a bowl to catch their juice. Set aside.

Heat the oil in a large, heavy-bottomed pan over medium heat. Add the onion, celery, garlic, and chili flakes. Sauté for about 5 minutes, stirring occasionally, then mix in the eggplant and sauté 5 more minutes. Add the tomatoes along with their juice. Reduce to low, cover, and simmer 10 minutes. Stir in the olives and capers and continue to cook 20–25 minutes, until the eggplant is tender but not mushy. Stir in the parsley and lemon juice until well combined. Serve at room temperature.

Each serving provides:

113	Calories	13 g	Carbohydrate
2 g	Protein	617 mg	Sodium
7 g	Fat	0 mg	Cholesterol
3 g	Dietary Fiber		

Cauliflower and Carrots with Tomato Mint Vinaigrette

VEGAN

Delicious and satisfying, this salad is easy to make and can be prepared well ahead of dinnertime. In Italy, a type of wild mint with a distinctive sweetness would be used here. If you cannot find truly delectable mint, include some fresh basil to enhance the flavor. This item is a wonderful addition to an antipasti presentation, but it can also be enjoyed as a side dish, served on individual lettuce leaves.

Yield: 8 antipasto servings

Low-sodium tomato juice	¼	cup
White wine vinegar	3	tablespoons
Tomato paste	1	tablespoon
Garlic	2	cloves, minced
Salt	¼	teaspoon
Pepper		Several grinds
Extra virgin olive oil	3	tablespoons
Fresh mint leaves, slivered	½	cup
Cauliflower	1½	pounds (1 large)
Carrots	½	pound (2 medium)
Red onion, minced	¼	cup

Whisk together the tomato juice, vinegar, tomato paste, garlic, salt, and pepper. When well combined, whisk in the olive oil in a thin stream. Stir in the mint leaves and set aside at room temperature, covered, for up to a few hours but at least 30 minutes, or store in the refrigerator for several days.

A few hours before you wish to serve the salad, remove and discard the leaves of the cauliflower and steam it whole for about 10 minutes, until fork-tender all the way through, but not soft and falling apart. Rinse with cold water and set aside in a colander to drain. Clean the carrots and cut crosswise into ¼-inch slices. Steam for 6–8 minutes, until just fork-tender. Rinse with cold water and drain well.

Cut the cooked cauliflower into bite-size pieces. In a large bowl, combine the cauliflower, carrots, and onion with the dressing and toss gently. Serve immediately.

Each serving provides:

89	Calories	9 g	Carbohydrate
2 g	Protein	108 mg	Sodium
5 g	Fat	0 mg	Cholesterol
3 g	Dietary Fiber		

Artichoke Bottoms Marinated with Chili Flakes and Balsamic Vinegar

VEGAN

In Italy, artichoke bottoms are sold fresh at the vegetable markets. Every morning large artichokes are trimmed of all their leaves and stems, and the resulting bottoms are placed in acidulated water. You simply purchase them as you would any other fresh vegetable. This recipe uses 5–6 large artichoke bottoms, totaling about ½ pound in weight, trimmed. In the United States, it is easiest to purchase water-packed canned artichoke bottoms.

Yield: 6 antipasto servings

Artichoke bottoms, water-packed	1	**14-ounce can**
Extra virgin olive oil	¼	**cup**
Green bell pepper, diced	¼	**cup**
Dried red chili flakes	¼	**teaspoon**
Garlic	5	**cloves, minced**
Balsamic vinegar	1	**tablespoon**

Drain and rinse the artichoke bottoms, then cut them into quarters. Heat the oil in a medium skillet over low heat. Add the green bell pepper and sauté for 2 minutes. Crush the chili flakes with a mortar and pestle, add, and continue to cook for 2 minutes. Add the garlic and sauté about 1 minute, then remove skillet from heat and pour contents into a shallow bowl. Stir in the balsamic vinegar, then add the artichoke pieces and toss to coat.

Allow to marinate at room temperature for about 1 hour before serving. You may prepare these several days in advance and keep them in the refrigerator, but bring them to room temperature before serving. Accompany this antipasto with crusty Italian bread.

Each serving provides:

96	Calories	4 g	Carbohydrate
1 g	Protein	181 mg	Sodium
9 g	Fat	0 mg	Cholesterol
1 g	Dietary Fiber		

Cardoon Fritters di Angello

The cardoon is a member of the thistle family, as is the artichoke. Its long stalks, 12–24 inches in length, resemble celery, though their flavor resembles the delicious cooked artichoke bottom. Cardoons grow wild in many areas and can be found in some Italian markets from November to March. Our dear friends, Joseph Angello and Bunnie Day, live on the Sacramento River and harvest them along the riverbanks. Joseph learned this recipe from his mother, and we enjoy it whenever cardoons come our way. If you grow conventional garden artichokes, you can harvest the tender inner stalks and substitute them for the cardoon stalks. We suggest these fritters as an antipasto, although they are so good you may wish to increase the serving size from 2 to 4 or 5 and call it a meal, accompanied by a salad.

Yield: 12 antipasto servings

Cardoons, trimmed	2	pounds
Eggs	2	large
Lowfat milk	¾	cup
Garlic	4	cloves, minced
Salt	½	teaspoon
Pepper		Several grinds
Unbleached flour	¾	cup
Baking soda	½	teaspoon
Olive oil	2	tablespoons

Prepare acidulated water in a large bowl by combining 2 quarts of cold water with 6 tablespoons of lemon juice or vinegar. Set aside near your work surface. Trim off and discard the cardoon leaves, then cut the trimmed stalk into 4-inch lengths. Drop these into the acidulated water to prevent darkening while you prepare the remaining stalks. Drain in a colander, then place in a large pot and cover with cold water. Put the lid on the pot and bring to a boil over high heat. Reduce slightly, set the lid ajar, and boil for about 1 hour, until the cardoons are fork-tender. This can be done ahead of time, in which case you should refrigerate the cooked stalks until needed.

Meanwhile, crack the eggs into a medium bowl and whisk slightly. Whisk in the milk, garlic, salt, and pepper, then the flour and baking soda. The batter will be somewhat thin. Drain the cooked cardoons thoroughly and cut them into ½-inch pieces. Drop them into the batter and stir to incorporate.

Heat 1 tablespoon of the oil in a large seasoned cast-iron or nonstick skillet over medium-high heat until a few drops of water sizzle when flicked into the pan. Use a large spoon to scoop up some cardoons and batter, and place in the hot pan to form 3-inch patties. Cook about 3–5 minutes until golden brown, then turn and brown the other side. Place fritters on a serving platter and keep warm in the oven while you cook the remaining ones. Add more oil to the skillet only as needed to prevent sticking. You will produce about 24 3-inch patties. Serve hot or at room temperature.

Each serving provides:

107	Calories	15 g	Carbohydrate
5 g	Protein	224 mg	Sodium
4 g	Fat	37 mg	Cholesterol
4 g	Dietary Fiber		

Fresh Mozzarella with Tomatoes and Basil

ALMOST INSTANT

This recipe calls for fresh mozzarella cheese made with buffalo's or cow's milk. It can be found water packed in the deli section of an Italian market. Seek it out, as no other cheese will do. This is a lovely dish to prepare in the summer when fresh tomatoes and basil abound. Pair this antipasto with a good crusty bread.

Yield: 8 antipasto servings

Fresh mozzarella	8	**ounces**
Tomatoes	1	**pound**
		(2 medium)
Extra virgin olive oil	2	**tablespoons**
Balsamic vinegar	1	**teaspoon**
Fresh basil leaves	12	
Salt	¼	**teaspoon**
Pepper		**Several grinds**

Cut the mozzarella and tomatoes into ¼-inch slices. Arrange them in an overlapping pattern on individual serving plates or on a platter. Drizzle with the olive oil, then the balsamic vinegar.

Stack the basil leaves and cut them crosswise into thin strips. Distribute them on top of the cheese and tomatoes, then add the salt and pepper. Serve at room temperature.

Each serving provides:

123	Calories	4 g	Carbohydrate
6 g	Protein	177 mg	Sodium
10 g	Fat	22 mg	Cholesterol
1 g	Dietary Fiber		

Summer Bread Salad

ALMOST INSTANT, VEGAN

This is our version of the classic Tuscan dish called panzanella.
*Preparing it is a terrific way to use up slightly stale bread. This
recipe calls for toasted bread cubes, which give the salad a satisfying
crunch. We have tried it with fresh, untoasted bread cubes, too, and
it is scrumptious both ways. In either case, you must start with an
unsliced loaf of chewy, robust country bread, not the sliced French
typically found in American supermarkets.*

Yield: 8 antipasto servings

Fresh or stale thick-crusted bread, cubed	4	**cups (about ¼ pound)**
Extra virgin olive oil	¼	**cup**
Red wine vinegar	¼	**cup**
Garlic	2	**cloves, minced**
Salt	¼	**teaspoon**
Pepper		**Several grinds**
Cucumber	1	**medium**
Fresh pear tomatoes	1	**pound**
Red onion, minced	¼	**cup**
Fresh basil leaves, slivered	¼	**cup**
Capers, drained	2	**tablespoons**

Cut the bread into ¾-inch cubes before measuring. Preheat
the oven to 350 degrees F. Spread the bread cubes in a single
layer on a baking sheet and toast in the oven until crisp and
lightly browned, about 8–10 minutes. Set aside to cool.

Meanwhile, whisk together the oil, vinegar, garlic, salt, and
pepper, and set aside. Peel the cucumber and cut in half lengthwise. Use a spoon to scrape out the seeds. Cut the cucumber
halves crosswise into ¼-inch slices. Set aside in a large bowl. Cut

the tomatoes in half crosswise and gently squeeze out the seed pockets. Dice the tomatoes and add them, with their juice, to the cucumbers. Add the onion, basil, capers, and dressing, and toss to combine. This much can be done ahead of time and held at room temperature for up to several hours.

Just before serving, add the bread cubes to the tomato mixture and toss to distribute everything evenly. Serve at room temperature.

Each serving provides:

127	Calories	13 g	Carbohydrate
2 g	Protein	206 mg	Sodium
8 g	Fat	0 mg	Cholesterol
2 g	Dietary Fiber		

Mixed Greens with Seasoned Croutons and Balsamic Vinaigrette

ALMOST INSTANT

Any mixture of baby greens may be used. A nice blend is butter lettuce, dandelion greens, radicchio, arugula, watercress, Belgian endive, and chicory. Experiment to find the combinations you most enjoy. Many markets sell a ready-mix of various greens that works well for this salad. You may toast your own seasoned croutons or use a commercially prepared variety.

Yield: 6 side-dish servings

Seasoned Croutons	1	**cup**
Extra virgin olive oil	2	**tablespoons**
Balsamic vinegar	1	**tablespoon**
Granulated garlic		**Scant ⅛ teaspoon**
Half-and-half	1	**teaspoon**
Mixed greens, loosely packed	8	**cups (about ¾ pound)**

Prepare the Seasoned Croutons according to the directions on page 33.

In a small bowl, whisk together the olive oil and vinegar. Add the garlic and half-and-half, whisk again, then set aside at room temperature.

Wash and dry the greens, then tear them into bite-size pieces. Place them in a large, shallow serving bowl. At this point, if you're not ready to serve the salad, the bowl of greens may be covered with a damp towel and placed in the refrigerator. Just before serving, briefly whisk the dressing to recombine and drizzle it over the greens. Toss to coat every leaf, then add the croutons and toss again. Serve immediately.

Each serving provides:

103	Calories	8 g	Carbohydrate
2 g	Protein	62 mg	Sodium
7 g	Fat	0 mg	Cholesterol
1 g	Dietary Fiber		

Caesar Salad

Caesar salad is thought to have been created in the mid 1920s by an Italian chef at Caesar's Place, his restaurant in Tijuana, Mexico. Most people enjoy it only in restaurants, but this simple recipe invites you to prepare it at home. The standard Worcestershire sauce contains anchovies. However, a low-sodium version is available that does not. If you include seafood in your diet, add 2 mashed anchovy fillets or 1 tablespoon of anchovy paste to the dressing.

Yield: 6 side-dish servings

Seasoned Croutons	1	**cup**
Egg*	1	**medium**
Romaine lettuce	1	**large head**
Garlic	2	**cloves, minced**
Fresh-squeezed lemon juice	3	**tablespoons**
Worcestershire sauce	1	**tablespoon**
Extra virgin olive oil	½	**cup**
Parmesan cheese, finely grated	½	**cup**

Prepare Seasoned Croutons according to the directions on page 33.

Wash and dry the lettuce, then tear it into bite-size pieces. Set aside. In a large bowl, whisk together the egg, garlic, lemon

*Some authorities suggest avoiding dishes made with raw eggs, due to the remote possibility of salmonella contamination. Immune-compromised individuals may wish to heed this advice. For more information, contact your local office of the U.S. Department of Agriculture.

juice, and Worcestershire sauce. Gradually add the oil in a thin stream, whisking as you do. Continue to whisk for a minute or two, then add the lettuce. Toss well to coat with the dressing. Add the croutons and Parmesan cheese, and toss again. Serve immediately.

Each serving provides:

271	Calories	9 g	Carbohydrate
7 g	Protein	221 mg	Sodium
24 g	Fat	42 mg	Cholesterol
2 g	Dietary Fiber		

Fennel and Radicchio Salad with Balsamic Vinaigrette

ALMOST INSTANT

This is a simple but unusual salad. The licorice flavor of the fennel is complemented by the bitterness of the radicchio, while olive oil and balsamic vinegar bind them together.

Yield: 4 side-dish servings

Extra virgin olive oil	2	**tablespoons**
Balsamic vinegar	1	**tablespoon**
Pepper		**Several grinds**
Fennel bulb, chopped	1½	**cups**
Radicchio, torn	2	**cups**
Parmesan cheese, finely grated	2	**tablespoons**
Butter lettuce leaves	4	**large**

In a small bowl, whisk together the oil, vinegar, and pepper. Place the fennel and radicchio in a bowl and toss with the dressing. Sprinkle on the cheese and toss again. Line 4 salad bowls with one lettuce leaf each and mound the fennel and radicchio on top. Serve immediately.

Each serving provides:

91	Calories	4 g	Carbohydrate
2 g	Protein	69 mg	Sodium
8 g	Fat	2 mg	Cholesterol
1 g	Dietary Fiber		

Antipasti and Salads

Potatoes and Artichokes with Mustard Caper Vinaigrette

VEGAN

This delicious antipasto combines many of the favorite flavors of the Mediterranean. Using fresh cooked artichokes instead of canned adds depth and subtlety of flavor—hallmarks of real Italian cooking. Trimming the artichokes is the most time-consuming preparation task for this dish, but it goes quickly once you get the hang of it. The marinated vegetables can be made several hours in advance and held at room temperature until serving time.

Yield: 6 antipasto servings

White wine vinegar	2	**tablespoons**
Dijon mustard	2	**teaspoons**
Garlic	2	**cloves, minced**
Extra virgin olive oil	3	**tablespoons**
Capers	2	**tablespoons, minced**
Artichokes	3	**pounds (6 medium)**
Tiny red potatoes	¾	**pound**
Red bell pepper, minced	⅓	**cup**
Fresh Italian parsley, minced	½	**cup**
Mixed salad greens, washed and dried	3	**cups, lightly packed**
Fresh lemon wedges	1	**per serving**

Stir together the vinegar, mustard, and garlic until well blended, then whisk in the olive oil. Stir in the capers. Set aside at room temperature while you prepare the vegetables.

Prepare acidulated water in a large bowl by combining 2 quarts of cold water with 6 tablespoons of lemon juice or vinegar. Set aside near your work surface.

Trim the artichokes, working with 1 artichoke at a time. Use your hands to snap off all outer leaves until you get down to the pale leaves at the center. The leaves may be steamed and eaten American style with melted butter or a good mayonnaise—or make a batch of Artichoke Pesto (see page 154). Use a sharp paring knife to cut off the leaf tips, leaving only the base and yellowish green leaves. Cut off ¼ inch of the stem end, then peel the stem and the bottom of each artichoke. Proceed until you have trimmed all the artichokes in this manner, dropping each artichoke into the acidulated water as you finish.

Remove the artichoke hearts from the water one at a time and quarter them from stem to top. Use a paring knife or melon baller to scrape out the fuzzy "choke" portion. Finally, slice each quarter lengthwise into thirds or fourths, depending on their size. You want wedges about ¼-inch thick. As you go, drop the artichoke pieces back into the acidulated water.

Scrub the potatoes well; do not peel. Slice them crosswise into ¼-inch-thick pieces. Pour an inch of water into the bottom of two medium-size saucepans. Put the potatoes in one, the artichokes in the other, and cover both pans. Place both pans over medium-high heat and cook the vegetables until fork-tender but not soft, about 6–8 minutes. Test frequently; the texture of the vegetables is important to the success of the dish.

When cooked, drain the artichokes and potatoes, and rinse with cold water. Drain thoroughly and toss together in a serving bowl, along with the bell pepper. Toss again with the dressing and set aside to marinate at room temperature for up to several hours, if you wish.

When ready to serve, toss the vegetable mixture with the parsley and greens. Serve with a wedge of lemon at each plate, and pass the pepper grinder.

Each serving provides:

192	Calories	29 g	Carbohydrate
6 g	Protein	232 mg	Sodium
8 g	Fat	0 mg	Cholesterol
9 g	Dietary Fiber		

Mushroom, Radish, and Celery Salad with Lemon and Garlic

ALMOST INSTANT, VEGAN

This simple dish offers lovely colors, a pleasing combination of textures, and light and lively flavor—a wonderful springtime combination! Be sure to use the celery's inner, yellowish stalks (the celery heart), which have a delicate, sweet flavor and aren't stringy.

Yield: 4 side-dish servings

Extra virgin olive oil	3	**tablespoons**
Fresh-squeezed lemon juice	3	**tablespoons**
Garlic	3	**cloves, minced**
Salt	¼	**teaspoon**
Pepper		**Several grinds**
Fresh Italian parsley, minced	¼	**cup**
Mushrooms, thinly sliced	2	**cups**
Red radishes, thinly sliced	1	**cup**
Celery hearts, thinly sliced	1	**cup**
Butter lettuce leaves	4	**large**

Whisk together the oil, lemon juice, garlic, salt, and pepper until well combined. Stir in the parsley and set aside at room temperature. Slice the vegetables and combine them in a bowl. Pour on the dressing and toss again. Serve immediately, or allow to stand at room temperature for an hour or two. Serve atop the lettuce leaves.

Each serving provides:

114	Calories	5 g	Carbohydrate
1 g	Protein	171 mg	Sodium
10 g	Fat	0 mg	Cholesterol
1 g	Dietary Fiber		

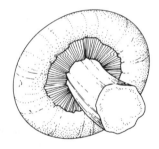 

Soups

When most Americans think of Italian soup, minestrone comes to mind—a chunky concoction of vegetables, beans, and macaroni in a tomato-laced broth. The *minestrone* category, however, includes many variations on the hearty soup theme. *Zuppa,* sometimes offered on restaurant menus, typically includes bread or croutons in its list of ingredients. The diverse and delicious array of Italian soups also includes simple, light broth preparations (*brodo*) and cream soups (*passato*). The umbrella term that includes all soups in Italy is *minestre.*

Soups are most often served as first courses, *primi piatti,* in Italian households, after the antipasto course. Many of the heartier soups, however, will also serve as delicious main courses when accompanied by antipasto, good bread, and salad. Parmesan or pecorino Romano cheese is typically offered to be grated onto soup, as desired.

Italians enjoy some of the same soups they eat hot in winter as cold or room-temperature soups in summer, often drizzled with fruity extra virgin olive oil and sprinkled with cheese.

Tips and Tools

- Wonderful homemade stock is a great soup enhancer. We provide a simple recipe for Italian Vegetable Stock on page 34. We strongly encourage you to keep a batch on hand in the refrigerator or freezer. However, the individual recipes also provide instructions for making instant soup stock from vegetable bouillon cubes.

- When a recipe calls for pureeing the soup, be sure to do it in small batches to avoid splattering the hot liquid.

- Most soups maintain their quality and may even improve in flavor for a day or two in the refrigerator.

- Since pasta will continue to absorb liquid after a soup is cooked, leftover soups that contain pasta may need to have broth added when they are reheated to achieve the right consistency.

- The only tools essential to wonderful soup-making are a large stockpot, a long-handled wooden spoon for stirring, and a ladle for serving.

Bread and Garlic Soup

ALMOST INSTANT, VEGAN

Pane cotto, *or bread soup, is another example of the simple, everyday dishes commonly prepared in Italian households. Use any good white or whole grain bread that is slightly stale. One of the great comfort foods, this soup takes little time to prepare, as long as you have good stock available. Serve it for lunch with bread and cheese, or as the first course of a dinner.*

Yield: 4 first-course servings

Italian Vegetable Stock*	**6**	**cups**
Garlic	**4**	**cloves, minced**
Stale bread, cubed	**1**	**cup**
Salt	**¼**	**teaspoon**
Pepper		**Several grinds**
Fresh Italian parsley, minced	**2**	**tablespoons**

Bring the stock to a boil in a saucepan over medium-high heat and add the garlic. Reduce the heat to medium and simmer for about 5 minutes to cook the garlic. Use a large wire whisk to

*If you do not have Italian Vegetable Stock on hand, make up a batch according to the directions on page 34, or dissolve 2 large low-sodium vegetable broth cubes in 6 cups of hot water.

stir in the bread cubes, salt, and pepper. Simmer 15–20 minutes, whisking occasionally as the bread breaks up and thickens the soup. Serve immediately in warm bowls, sprinkling the parsley on top.

Each serving provides:

64	Calories	13 g	Carbohydrate
1 g	Protein	459 mg	Sodium
0 g	Fat	0 mg	Cholesterol
0 g	Dietary Fiber		

Tortellini in Tomato Porcini Broth with Escarole

ALMOST INSTANT

So many good stuffed pasta products are available in our markets that we don't always need to make them from scratch. Experiment with different brands of fresh cheese-stuffed tortellini until you find a favorite, then keep some on hand for convenient dishes such as this one. A delicious, rich-tasting broth is essential to its success, so homemade stock is preferable to one made from bouillon cubes. If escarole is unavailable, you could substitute arugula or another slightly bitter green.

Yield: 4 first-course servings

Italian Vegetable Stock°	4	**cups**
Dried porcini mushrooms	⅓	**ounce**
Dried tomatoes	½	**cup**
Garlic	1	**clove, minced**
Dry sherry	1	**tablespoon**
Salt		**A pinch**
Cheese-stuffed tortellini, fresh	6	**ounces**
Escarole leaves, slivered	2	**cups**
Parmesan cheese, finely grated	2	**tablespoons**

Bring the stock to a simmer in a large saucepan over high heat. Add the mushrooms, tomatoes, garlic, and sherry, and cover the pan. Turn off the heat and allow the mixture to steep for

---

°If you do not have any Italian Vegetable Stock on hand, make up a batch using the recipe on page 34, or dissolve 1½ large low-sodium vegetable broth cubes in 4 cups of hot water.

30 minutes. Strain the broth through a paper coffee filter or several layers of cheesecloth, pressing with a wooden spoon to remove as much liquid as possible. If you wish, you may save the reconstituted mushrooms and tomatoes for another use, such as Dried Tomato and Olive Pesto (page 44).

Taste the broth and season with salt, if necessary. The broth may be made ahead of time and stored in a closed container in the refrigerator for up to a few days. When you are ready to make the soup, bring the broth to a boil over high heat. Add the tortellini and escarole, and return to a boil. Reduce heat to medium and simmer for about 10 minutes, until tortellini are al dente. Ladle equal portions of tortellini into 4 warmed bowls, and cover with broth. Sprinkle each serving with Parmesan and serve very hot.

Each serving provides:

216	Calories	17 g	Carbohydrate
10 g	Protein	615 mg	Sodium
4 g	Fat	25 mg	Cholesterol
1 g	Dietary Fiber		

Spiced Broth with Spinach, Mushrooms, Eggs, and Cheese

ALMOST INSTANT

This pretty, warming soup makes a delicious light entrée or first course. The traditional version, called stracciatelli, *uses meat stock and prosciutto for flavoring. Our version is quite delectable without them. Perfectly fresh, succulent spinach is essential to the success of this dish.*

Yield: 4 first-course servings

Yellow onion	½	**small**
Mushrooms	4	**ounces**
Italian Vegetable Stock*	5	**cups**
Tomato paste	2	**tablespoons**
Pepper		**Several grinds**
Fresh spinach	6	**ounces**
Eggs	2	**medium**
Ground cinnamon	⅛	**teaspoon**
Freshly grated nutmeg	⅛	**teaspoon**
Salt		**A pinch**
Parmesan cheese, finely grated	¼	**cup**

Slice the onion and mushrooms very thinly. In a large saucepan, combine the stock, onion, mushrooms, tomato paste, and pepper. Bring to a simmer over high heat, then reduce the heat to medium-low and simmer, uncovered, 10 minutes. Meanwhile,

---

*If you do not have Italian Vegetable Stock on hand, make up a batch using the recipe on page 34, or dissolve 1½ large vegetable broth cubes in 5 cups of hot water and add a minced clove of garlic.

Soups

wash the spinach well, discard the stems, and cut the leaves into thin slivers. Set aside. Lightly beat the eggs with the cinnamon, nutmeg, and salt until well combined, then stir in the cheese. Pour the egg mixture in a slow, steady stream into the simmering soup, stirring with a fork to create ribbons of egg in the broth. Turn off the heat and stir in the spinach. It will wilt at once. Serve immediately.

Each serving provides:

121	Calories	13 g	Carbohydrate
7 g	Protein	454 mg	Sodium
4 g	Fat	111 mg	Cholesterol
2 g	Dietary Fiber		

Tuscan White Bean Puree
with Garlic and Fresh Sage

This soup, known as passato de fagioli, *is pure comfort food! In Italy, it would probably be laced with pancetta or prosciutto. However, we find that the fresh sage, garlic, Parmesan, and fruity olive oil carry the dish quite well on their own. Reserve some whole sage leaves for a pretty garnish, if you wish.*

Yield: 6 first-course servings

Dried cannellini beans	1½	**cups**
Garlic	3	**cloves, minced**
Salt	¼	**teaspoon**
Extra virgin olive oil	4	**tablespoons**
Fresh sage leaves, slivered	¼	**cup**
Parmesan cheese, finely grated	⅓	**cup**
Pepper		**Several grinds**

Sort the beans and place them in a large pan or bowl. Cover with boiling water, put on a lid, and soak for several hours, then drain in a colander.

Place the soaked beans in a stockpot with 7 cups of cold water. Add 2 minced cloves of garlic and the salt, and bring to a boil over high heat. Reduce heat to medium and simmer 1–1½ hours, or until the beans are very tender.

Puree the beans in small batches and return the puree to the pot. If it seems too thick, you may add stock, milk, or water 1 tablespoon at a time until you achieve the proper consistency. It should be thick and hearty, so beware of thinning it too much.

Heat the olive oil briefly over medium-low heat in a small skillet. Stir in the remaining garlic clove and the sage. Cook, stirring constantly, for about 1 minute. You want the garlic and sage to flavor the oil, but don't let the garlic brown. Pour this mixture into the bean puree, using a rubber spatula to remove all the flavorful oil from the pan. Add Parmesan and a good deal of black pepper, and stir to incorporate thoroughly. Heat through over very low heat and serve hot.

Each serving provides:

271	Calories	31 g	Carbohydrate
14 g	Protein	180 mg	Sodium
11 g	Fat	4 mg	Cholesterol
3 g	Dietary Fiber		

Cream of Fennel Soup
with Broccoli Rabe

Fennel's licorice flavor complements the bitterness of broccoli rabe. This is sure to become one of your favorite winter soups.

Yield: 4 main-course servings

Unsalted butter	2	**tablespoons**
Dry sherry	2	**tablespoons**
Yellow onion	1	**medium, minced**
Italian Vegetable Stock*	2	**cups**
Fennel bulb	1	**pound (1 medium)**
Broccoli rabe	½	**pound, chopped**
Lowfat milk	2	**cups**
Salt	¼	**teaspoon**
Pepper		**Several grinds**

Melt the butter in a large skillet over medium-low heat. Add the sherry and onion, and sauté for 10 minutes. Trim off the stalks of the fennel and slice the bulb in half. Cut out the small center core and discard. Chop the bulb, retaining the stalks for another use, such as soup stock. Add the stock and fennel to the skillet and increase the heat to bring the contents to a simmer. Cover, reduce heat to medium, and simmer for 20 minutes, stirring occasionally.

*If you do not have Italian Vegetable Stock on hand, make up a batch according to the directions on page 34, or dissolve ½ of a large low-sodium vegetable broth cube in 2 cups of hot water.

Coarsely chop the broccoli rabe and separate the stem ends from the leaf section. Add the stems to the skillet and continue to simmer, covered, for 10 minutes. Finely chop the leaf section and set aside.

Puree the fennel mixture in a blender or food processor in several batches to avoid splattering. Transfer to a stockpot and add the milk, salt, pepper, and leaf section of the broccoli rabe. Heat through over medium heat for about 5 minutes, being careful not to let it boil. Serve immediately, with Parmesan cheese, if desired.

Each serving provides:

188	Calories	21 g	Carbohydrate
7 g	Protein	345 mg	Sodium
9 g	Fat	26 mg	Cholesterol
4 g	Dietary Fiber		

Cream of Mushroom Soup with Marsala

Nutmeg and a small quantity of dried porcini mushrooms enrich this delicious version of mushroom soup. Serve with thick-crusted country bread and a tart leafy salad for lunch or a light supper.

Yield: 4 main-course servings

Italian Vegetable Stock*	2	**cups**
Dried porcini mushrooms	1/3	**ounce**
Whole milk	1 1/4	**cups**
Unsalted butter	2	**tablespoons**
White onion	1	**medium, minced**
Celery, including leaves	1	**inner rib, minced**
Fresh Italian parsley, minced	2	**tablespoons**
Garlic	1	**clove, minced**
Dried thyme	1/4	**teaspoon**
Tomato paste	2	**tablespoons**
Unbleached flour	2	**tablespoons**
Mushrooms	3/4	**pound, thinly sliced**
Salt	1/4	**teaspoon**
Pepper		**Several grinds**
Marsala	1/2	**cup**
Heavy cream	1/4	**cup**
Freshly grated nutmeg	1	**teaspoon**

*If you do not have any Italian Vegetable Stock on hand, make up a batch using the recipe on page 34, or dissolve 1/2 of a large low-sodium vegetable broth cube in 2 cups of hot water.

In a small saucepan, heat the stock over medium-high heat until it is steaming. Add the dried mushrooms, cover, and turn off the heat. Allow to steep for 30 minutes. Strain through a paper coffee filter and set the resulting broth aside. If gritty, rinse the mushrooms well under a thin stream of running water. Finely mince the reconstituted mushrooms and set them aside.

Combine the broth and milk in a saucepan and heat to steaming over medium-low heat. Meanwhile, melt the butter in a stockpot over medium heat. Add the onion, celery, parsley, garlic, and thyme, and sauté, stirring frequently, 5 minutes. Stir in the tomato paste until incorporated, then stir in the flour. Add about 1 cup of the hot broth mixture and stir until blended and slightly thickened. Stir in the remainder of the broth, then the sliced mushrooms, porcini, salt, and pepper. Bring to a simmer over medium-high heat, cover, reduce heat to medium-low, and simmer 30 minutes. Remove the lid to stir contents 2 or 3 times during this half hour.

Puree half the mixture in a blender or food processor in small batches and return to the pot. Stir in the Marsala, cream, and nutmeg, and heat through for 2–3 minutes. Serve hot, passing additional nutmeg, if you wish.

Each serving provides:

257	Calories	21 g	Carbohydrate
6 g	Protein	320 mg	Sodium
15 g	Fat	48 mg	Cholesterol
2 g	Dietary Fiber		

Rice, Pea, and Mushroom Soup with Fresh Oregano

VEGAN

This soup was inspired by Risi e Bisi *(Rice and Peas), a beloved Venetian dish. Our version is made from simple, inexpensive ingredients available year-round. Fix it anytime you want a meal that is quick to prepare, hearty, and warming. The perfect accompaniments would be a coarse country bread, served with Seasoned Olive Oil (page 46), and a crisp, tart salad. For an extra special treat, make the soup with field mushrooms (such as chanterelles or porcini) instead of, or in addition to, supermarket button mushrooms.*

Yield: 4 main-course servings

Olive oil	2	**tablespoons**
Yellow onion	1	**medium, diced**
Dried rosemary	½	**teaspoon, crushed**
Mushrooms	½	**pound, sliced**
Garlic	3	**cloves, minced**
Salt	½	**teaspoon**
Pepper		**Several grinds**
Italian Vegetable Stock*	7	**cups**
Long-grain white rice	1	**cup**
Frozen shelled peas	2	**cups**
Fresh oregano, minced	2	**tablespoons**

*If you do not have any Italian Vegetable Stock on hand, make up a batch using the directions on page 34, or dissolve 2 large low-sodium vegetable broth cubes in 7 cups of hot water.

Heat the olive oil over medium heat in a stockpot. Sauté the onion with the rosemary for 5 minutes, stirring often. The onion will begin to brown. Add the mushrooms, garlic, salt, and pepper, and stir and sauté about 2 minutes, then add the stock. Cover and bring to a boil over high heat, then stir in the rice. Return to a boil, reduce heat to medium and simmer, uncovered, 15 minutes, stirring occasionally. Add the peas and oregano, and continue to cook until rice is tender, about 5 minutes. Serve hot.

Each serving provides:

366	Calories	64 g	Carbohydrate
9 g	Protein	666 mg	Sodium
8 g	Fat	0 mg	Cholesterol
4 g	Dietary Fiber		

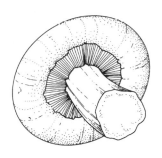

Turnip, Chard, and Rice Soup with Ricotta Cheese

This stunning soup is sure to please even die-hard turnip detractors. They won't know what they're eating, only that it tastes wonderful. We have made a meal of it with only hearty bread, olives, and Gorgonzola cheese as accompaniments. Be sure to choose small turnips for this dish. The larger ones tend to have stringy fibers that would ruin the soup's texture.

Yield: 6 main-course servings

Red bell pepper	1	medium
Turnips	1	pound (6 small)
Swiss chard	¾	pound
Unsalted butter	2	tablespoons
Yellow onion	1	medium, diced
Salt	½	teaspoon
Pepper		Several grinds
Italian Vegetable Stock*	6	cups
Long-grain white rice	½	cup
Part-skim ricotta cheese	1	cup
Half-and-half	2	tablespoons
Dry sherry	2	tablespoons
Freshly grated nutmeg	1	teaspoon

Remove the seeds, stem, and white membrane from the pepper and dice small. Peel the turnips and dice small. Remove the chard leaves from the stems. Rinse the stems and slice cross-

---

*If you do not have any Italian Vegetable Stock on hand, make up a batch using the recipe on page 34, or dissolve 2 large low-sodium vegetable broth cubes in 6 cups of hot water.

wise into thin slivers, discarding any badly discolored portions. Chop the leaves and set them aside.

Melt the butter in a stockpot over medium-high heat, but don't allow it to brown. Quickly add the bell pepper, turnips, chard stems, onion, salt, and pepper. Sauté, stirring frequently, for 12 minutes. It is fine if the vegetables begin to brown, but stir them to prevent scorching. Add the stock and increase the heat to high. Bring to a boil, stir in the rice, reduce heat to medium, and simmer for about 20 minutes, until turnips and rice are tender.

Meanwhile, thin the ricotta by whisking it with the half-and-half and sherry in a small bowl, then whisk in the nutmeg. When the soup is ready, ladle about a cup of the hot broth into the ricotta mixture and stir to combine. Turn off the heat, pour the ricotta mixture into the soup, add the chard leaves, and stir to incorporate. With a wooden spoon, mash some of the turnip pieces against the side of the pot. Just a few mashing strokes will do to thicken the broth a little. Cover and allow the soup to stand 5 minutes before serving.

Each serving provides:

222	Calories	29 g	Carbohydrate
8 g	Protein	572 mg	Sodium
8 g	Fat	25 mg	Cholesterol
2 g	Dietary Fiber		

Winter Squash and Cauliflower Soup with Tomatoes, Rosemary, and Marsala

VEGAN

This tangy/sweet soup hits the spot when autumn's chill and the new crop of winter squashes simultaneously arrive. Once the squash is peeled and diced, most of the work is done. Bread, cheese, and a bowl of olives round out the meal in an authentic manner. One large acorn squash (about 1½ pounds) will yield about 4 cups of diced flesh, but Hubbard or butternut squash can also be used.

Yield: 6 main-course servings

Winter squash	1½	pounds
Olive oil	1	tablespoon
Yellow onion, diced	1	medium
Dried red chili flakes	¼	teaspoon
Garlic	5	cloves, minced
Dried rosemary	2	teaspoons
Salt	⅛	teaspoon
Italian Vegetable Stock°	4	cups
Whole tomatoes	1	28-ounce can
Cauliflower, diced	2	cups
Dried small shell pasta	¾	cup
Marsala wine	⅓	cup

°If you do not have Italian Vegetable Stock on hand, make up a batch using the recipe on page 34, or dissolve 1½ large low-sodium vegetable broth cubes in 4 cups of hot water.

Cut the squash in half and scrape out the seeds and stringy pulp. Peel the squash and dice the flesh to measure 4 cups. Heat the olive oil in a stockpot over medium-high heat for a moment, then add the onion and chili flakes. Stir and sauté about 2 minutes, then stir in the squash, garlic, rosemary, and salt. Sauté about 7 minutes, stirring frequently, until the squash and onions are beginning to brown. Add the stock and the tomatoes with their juice. Cover and bring to a boil over high heat. Stir in the cauliflower, pasta, and Marsala, and bring back to a boil over high heat. Reduce heat to medium-high to maintain a strong simmer and cook about 12 minutes, until cauliflower is fork-tender and pasta is al dente. Serve very hot in warmed bowls.

Each serving provides:

186	Calories	34 g	Carbohydrate
5 g	Protein	388 mg	Sodium
3 g	Fat	0 mg	Cholesterol
4 g	Dietary Fiber		

Winter Vegetable Minestrone with Rosemary and Rice

VEGAN

Minestrone is the thick, substantial soup enjoyed all over Italy. In the northern regions, the cooks prefer rice to pasta and often make their minestrone with it. This fantasia *utilizes* riso, *winter vegetables, and rosemary, one of the few herbs that can be enjoyed fresh from the winter garden.*

Yield: 6 main-course servings

Dried cannellini beans	½	**cup**
Italian Vegetable Stock°	6	**cups**
Russet potatoes	1	**pound (2 large)**
Carrots	½	**pound (2 large)**
Whole pear tomatoes	1	**16-ounce can**
Olive oil	2	**tablespoons**
Yellow onion	1	**medium, diced**
Celery	2	**ribs, diced**
Garlic	3	**cloves, minced**
Arborio rice, uncooked	½	**cup**
Swiss chard	1	**pound, chopped**
Dried sage	1	**teaspoon**
Fresh rosemary, minced	1	**tablespoon**
Salt	¼	**teaspoon**
Pepper		**Several grinds**

°If you do not have Italian Vegetable Stock on hand, make up a batch according to the directions on page 34, or dissolve 2 large low-sodium vegetable broth cubes in 6 cups of hot water.

Sort the beans and place in a large pan or bowl. Cover with boiling water, put on a lid, and soak for several hours, then drain in a colander and set aside. Bring the stock to a boil in a large stockpot over high heat. Add the beans, lower the heat to medium-high, and simmer for 40 minutes.

Scrub the potatoes and carrots, peel if desired, then dice and add them to the stockpot along with 2 cups of hot water. Drain the tomato liquid into the stockpot and put the tomatoes into a bowl to catch their juice as you coarsely chop them. Add tomatoes to the pot, increase the heat to high, and bring to a boil. Reduce heat to medium-high and continue to cook for 30 minutes.

Meanwhile, heat the olive oil in a large skillet over medium heat and sauté the onion, celery, and garlic for about 7 minutes. Stir the sautéed vegetables into the stockpot, along with the rice. Add 2 more cups of hot water, the chard, sage, rosemary, salt, and pepper, stirring to combine. Continue to cook 20–25 minutes until the rice is tender. Stir occasionally. Serve, passing Parmesan cheese, if you wish.

Each serving provides:

297	Calories	55 g	Carbohydrate
9 g	Protein	580 mg	Sodium
5 g	Fat	0 mg	Cholesterol
5 g	Dietary Fiber		

Classic Pasta, Bean, and Vegetable Minestrone

We first learned of this hearty soup, known in Italian as pasta e fagioli, *from the Ferrannini family. Their version calls for prosciutto, an Italian ham, which lends a smoky character. Here we have substituted dried tomatoes to enhance the flavor of this favorite comfort food. The dried small tube pasta is frequently sold as "salad macaroni" in American markets.*

Yield: 6 main-course servings

Dried cannellini beans	1½	**cups**
Dried tomatoes, minced	2	**tablespoons**
Olive oil	2	**tablespoons**
Yellow onion	1	**medium, diced**
Carrot	1	**medium**
Celery	1	**rib, diced**
Garlic	3	**cloves, minced**
Italian Vegetable Stock*	5	**cups**
Dried small tube pasta	8	**ounces**
Salt	¼	**teaspoon**
Pepper		**Several grinds**
Fresh Italian parsley, minced	¼	**cup**
Romano cheese, finely grated	¼	**cup**

*If you do not have Italian Vegetable Stock on hand, make up a batch according to the directions on page 34, or dissolve 2 large low-sodium vegetable broth cubes in 5 cups of hot water.

Sort the beans and place them in a large pan or bowl. Cover with boiling water, put on a lid, and soak for several hours, then drain in a colander and set aside. Heat 5 cups of fresh water to a boil, add the drained beans, return to a boil, and cook for about 30 minutes over medium heat. Reconstitute the dried tomatoes if they are too dry to mince by soaking for 15–30 minutes in hot water. Drain well, then mince them. Set aside.

Meanwhile, heat the oil in a skillet over medium-high heat and add the onion, carrot, celery, and garlic. Sauté until tender, about 10 minutes, stirring frequently. Add the stock to the beans along with the dried tomatoes, sautéed vegetables, salt, and pepper. Bring to a boil over medium-high heat; reduce heat slightly and cook for 15 minutes until the beans are almost tender. Add the pasta plus 1 cup of hot water and continue to cook for 12–15 minutes, until pasta is al dente. Stir in the parsley just before serving. Pass the grated cheese.

The soup should be very thick. If you have leftovers, you will need to add some water or stock before reheating.

Each serving provides:

412	Calories	69 g	Carbohydrate
19 g	Protein	357 mg	Sodium
7 g	Fat	3 mg	Cholesterol
5 g	Dietary Fiber		

Basil Pesto Minestrone with Cabbage and Dried Tomatoes

You may use the Basil Pesto recipe in this book and freeze the surplus, or purchase a commercially prepared variety. We like to use pastina—small pasta stars or bow ties—but broken spaghetti will also work. This is a delicious soup that can be made quickly, provided you have the ingredients on hand.

Yield: 4 main-course servings

Dried tomatoes, minced	¼	**cup**
Olive oil	1	**tablespoon**
Marsala wine	3	**tablespoons**
Garlic	2	**cloves, minced**
Yellow onion	1	**medium, diced**
Celery	2	**ribs, diced**
Italian Vegetable Stock*	4	**cups**
Green cabbage, chopped	3	**cups**
Pastina	⅔	**cup**
Basil Pesto (see page 134)	¼	**cup**
Lowfat milk	½	**cup**

*If you do not have Italian Vegetable Stock on hand, make up a batch according to the directions on page 34, or dissolve 1 large low-sodium vegetable broth cube in 4 cups of hot water.

If the dried tomatoes are too dry to mince, soak them for 15–30 minutes in hot water. Drain well, then mince. Set aside.

Place the oil and Marsala in a stockpot over medium heat. Add the garlic, onion, and celery, and stir to combine. Sauté for about 5 minutes, stirring occasionally, then add the stock, dried tomatoes, and cabbage. Increase the heat to medium-high and simmer for 10 minutes, until the vegetables are tender. Add the pastina and ½ cup of hot water, then increase the heat slightly to bring to a boil. Cook 5–6 minutes, stirring occasionally so the pasta does not stick to the bottom of the pan. When the pastina is al dente, add the pesto and milk, heat through, and serve immediately.

Each serving provides:

303	Calories	37 g	Carbohydrate
8 g	Protein	342 mg	Sodium
13 g	Fat	4 mg	Cholesterol
3 g	Dietary Fiber		

Cranberry Bean Minestrone with Fresh Sage and Marjoram

VEGAN

Cranberry beans, also known as borlotti beans, are popular in Italian cooking. The bean is pink with red speckles, similar to a pinto bean, which may be substituted if you cannot find cranberry beans. This minestrone is reminiscent of the country soups served in the hillside villages of Tuscany.

Yield: 4 main-course servings

Dried cranberry beans	1	**cup**
Italian Vegetable Stock*	4	**cups**
Olive oil	2	**tablespoons**
Yellow onion	1	**medium, chopped**
Celery	2	**ribs, chopped**
Garlic	3	**cloves, minced**
Pear tomatoes	1	**14½-ounce can**
Fresh sage leaves, minced	2	**tablespoons**
Fresh marjoram leaves, minced	1	**tablespoon**
Freshly grated nutmeg	¼	**teaspoon**
Salt	½	**teaspoon**
Pepper		**Several grinds**

*If you do not have Italian Vegetable Stock on hand, make up a batch according to the directions on page 34, or dissolve 1 large low-sodium vegetable broth cube in 4 cups of hot water.

Sort the beans and place in a large pan or bowl. Cover with boiling water, put on a lid, and soak for several hours, then drain in a colander and set aside. Heat the stock over medium high heat in a large stockpot and add the beans. Bring to a boil, reduce heat to medium-low, and simmer with lid ajar for about 45 minutes, until beans are almost tender.

Meanwhile, place the olive oil in a skillet over medium heat. Add the onion, celery, and garlic, and sauté for about 5 minutes, until the onion is translucent. Chop the tomatoes in a bowl or use your hands to break them up, then add them with their juice to the beans. Stir in the onion mixture, sage, marjoram, nutmeg, salt, and pepper. Cook over medium-low heat, uncovered, for about 30 minutes, stirring occasionally. Serve immediately.

Each serving provides:

289	Calories	45 g	Carbohydrate
11 g	Protein	635 mg	Sodium
8 g	Fat	0 mg	Cholesterol
7 g	Dietary Fiber		

Eggplant and Garbanzo Minestrone with Fresh Basil

VEGAN

Unpretentious and delicious, this soup hits the spot on chilly evenings. It makes a wonderfully satisfying meal with the addition of a good bread, leafy salad, and wine. You may use rinsed canned beans rather than freshly cooked ones, if you wish.

Yield: 6 main-course servings

Olive oil	2	**tablespoons**
Yellow onion	1	**medium, diced**
Garlic	3	**cloves, minced**
Red bell pepper	½	**medium, diced**
Dried marjoram	2	**teaspoons**
Eggplant	1	**large, peeled and chopped**
Salt	¼	**teaspoon**
Pepper		**Several grinds**
Whole tomatoes	1	**28-ounce can**
Italian Vegetable Stock°	4	**cups**
Cooked garbanzo beans	2	**cups**
Dried pastina	½	**cup**
Fresh basil leaves, slivered	1	**cup**

°If you do not have Italian Vegetable Stock on hand, make up a batch using the recipe on page 34, or dissolve 1½ large vegetable broth cubes in 4 cups of hot water.

Heat the olive oil in a large stockpot over medium heat. Add the onion and garlic, and sauté 2 minutes, then add the bell pepper and marjoram. Sauté 5 minutes, stirring occasionally. Add the eggplant, salt, and pepper. Sauté 5 minutes longer, stirring occasionally. Add the tomatoes with their juice, along with the stock and garbanzo beans, and bring to a simmer over high heat. Reduce heat to medium-low, cover, and cook 15 minutes. Increase heat to medium-high to achieve a good boil and add the pastina. Cook until the pastina is al dente, 5–10 minutes, depending on its size. Stir in the basil and serve hot, passing Parmesan cheese if you wish.

Each serving provides:

263	Calories	44 g	Carbohydrate
9 g	Protein	429 mg	Sodium
7 g	Fat	0 mg	Cholesterol
5 g	Dietary Fiber		

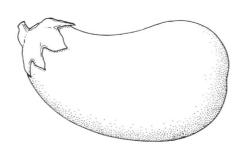

Essential Sauces

The sauces of Italy are renowned worldwide for their diversity and extraordinary flavor. Best known are pasta sauces, but in Italy sauces also appear frequently with polenta, risotto, meats, and vegetables.

This chapter is a sampler of our favorite classic Italian sauces and includes many of the best regional sauces. Though many people suppose pasta with tomato sauce to be a staple of Italian cooking, Northern Italians rarely use tomato sauce. There, the Alpine influence has resulted in a long tradition of creamy sauces.

The sauces included here lend themselves to many uses, and we have provided serving suggestions in the recipe introductions. Some of these sauces are ingredients in other dishes in this book.

Throughout Italy, sauces are used to enhance, not smother, the flavors of various foods. Italian sauces are either rich and creamy or robust with spices, and a small amount delivers a lot of flavor. Therefore, we recommend you begin with the highest quality pasta, polenta, rice, and vegetables, and add the sauce with a light hand.

Tips and Tools

- Cooked sauces generally come together quickly. When you melt the butter or heat the olive oil, have your other ingredients close at hand.

- Reheat cream sauces in a double boiler or very briefly in a microwave oven. Placing a cream sauce over a direct flame can cause scorching.

- When combining pasta with raw sauces such as walnut sauce or pesto, drain the cooked pasta quickly and toss it while still very hot with the sauce. Cold or extremely thick pestos should be warmed and thinned slightly with a tablespoon or two of the hot pasta-cooking water before combining with the pasta.

- Always serve sauced dishes on warmed plates to maintain an appetizing temperature.

- Successful sauce-making requires a heavy-bottomed pan to distribute the heat evenly and prevent scorching.

- A wire whisk is essential for achieving a smooth texture in cream sauces.

- Traditionally, pesto ingredients were ground together by hand using a mortar and pestle—and plenty of elbow grease. In our kitchens, however, we use a food processor to do the same job in minutes.

Fresh Tomato Coulis

ALMOST INSTANT, VEGAN

This versatile sauce is delicious with pasta or grilled polenta, or in any dish where a light but chunky tomato sauce is desired. We provide detailed instructions to familiarize you with the simple method of preparing Italian-style tomato sauce. Over the years, you will come up with many tasty variations on this basic theme. Let your imagination take you for a ride as you experiment fearlessly. You might make a delicious discovery!

Yield: 2 cups

Fresh pear tomatoes (or 1 28-ounce can pear tomatoes)	**3**	**pounds**
Olive oil	**1**	**tablespoon**
Garlic	**2**	**cloves, minced**
Herbs, fresh or dried		**Amounts vary**
Salt	**½**	**teaspoon**
Pepper		**A few grinds**

If using fresh tomatoes, put several quarts of water on to boil in a large pot. Blanch, peel, and seed the tomatoes according to the directions on page 27. Alternately, drain the juice from the canned whole tomatoes and reserve for another use (such as soup). Coarsely chop the tomatoes into a bowl.

Heat the oil in a heavy-bottomed skillet. Stir and sauté the minced garlic for about 1 minute, then pour in the tomatoes all at once. Cook over medium-high heat, stirring frequently, about 5 minutes. The tomatoes will break apart and liquefy a bit. Add a tablespoon or so of fresh oregano or basil leaves, or smaller amounts of fresh rosemary or thyme. Any combination of the above will be authentic and tasty. If using dried herbs, begin with a teaspoon or so each of oregano and/or basil, perhaps ¼ teaspoon of the stronger-flavored thyme and rosemary. Salt and pepper the sauce at this stage, using the recommended amounts as a guide, but varying to your own taste. Simmer only a few minutes longer over medium-high heat, until the liquid has reduced considerably. You'll know by the look of it when you've achieved the right consistency.

Some hints for variations: When adding the herbs, you can include a tablespoon or two of capers or chopped olives. A few ounces of red wine, sherry, or brandy will create a distinctive effect. In place of the herbs, you can stir in a few tablespoons of prepared Basil Pesto (see page 134).

Note: This recipe yields enough sauce for 12 ounces dried pasta, cooked and drained.

Each ½ cup provides:

86	Calories	12 g	Carbohydrate
2 g	Protein	289 mg	Sodium
4 g	Fat	0 mg	Cholesterol
3 g	Dietary Fiber		

Chunky Tomato Cream Sauce

ALMOST INSTANT

In keeping with the Italian tradition, this sauce calls for a small amount of heavy cream to develop its richness. If you prefer a slightly lighter version, substitute light sour cream or nonfat yogurt. We enjoy this sauce over polenta or pasta.

Yield: 2 cups

Olive oil	1	tablespoon
Garlic	2	cloves, minced
Whole pear tomatoes	1	28-ounce can
Dried oregano	¼	teaspoon
Capers, drained	2	tablespoons, minced
Heavy cream	2	tablespoons

Heat the olive oil in a large heavy-bottomed skillet over medium heat and sauté the garlic for about a minute. Chop the tomatoes into a bowl and add them, with their juice, to the skillet. Add the oregano, crumbling it between your palms. Increase heat to medium-high and sauté for about 10 minutes, until most of the liquid has evaporated. Reduce to medium and stir in the capers, then the heavy cream. Serve immediately, or use as specified in a recipe. The sauce will keep in the refrigerator for several days.

Note: This recipe yields enough sauce for 12 ounces dried pasta, cooked and drained.

Each ½ cup provides:

107	Calories	11 g	Carbohydrate
1 g	Protein	424 mg	Sodium
7 g	Fat	11 mg	Cholesterol
1 g	Dietary Fiber		

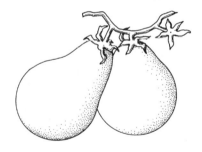

Puttanesca Sauce

ALMOST INSTANT, VEGAN

Hot, spicy, *and* sassy *are three words that describe this sauce.
Puttanesca sauce usually contains anchovies, but we find our vegan
version delicious. Serve it tossed with spiral pasta, over grilled
polenta, or even with scrambled eggs. If you are preparing this sauce
in tomato season, substitute 3 pounds of fresh tomatoes for the
canned ones. Blanch and chop them coarsely into a bowl to catch the
juices, then proceed with the recipe.*

Yield: 4 cups

Olive oil	1	**tablespoon**
Garlic	3	**cloves, minced**
Dried red chili flakes	½	**teaspoon**
Pear tomatoes	1	**28-ounce can**
Dry oil-cured black olives, pitted and chopped	½	**cup**
Capers	2	**tablespoons**

Heat the olive oil over medium-low heat in a large skillet. Add
the garlic and chili flakes, then sauté 1–2 minutes. Add the
tomatoes, with their juice, and continue to cook over medium-

high heat for 15 minutes, until the liquid has begun to evaporate. Add the olives and capers, and continue to cook for 10 minutes. The sauce will be very thick and dark.

Note: This recipe yields enough sauce for 1½ pounds dried pasta, cooked and drained.

Each ½ cup provides:

65	Calories	6 g	Carbohydrate
1 g	Protein	443 mg	Sodium
5 g	Fat	0 mg	Cholesterol
1 g	Dietary Fiber		

Roasted Tomato and Onion Sauce with Fresh Sage

ALMOST INSTANT, VEGAN

Roasting lends the tomatoes and onion a smoky quality that complements the earthy flavor of fresh sage. This is a terrific sauce for any stuffed pasta or plain noodle, and can be made a few days ahead of time. It also freezes well.

Yield: 2 cups

Fresh pear tomatoes	2	**pounds**
White onion	1	**large**
Garlic	2	**cloves**
Olive oil	1	**tablespoon**
Fresh sage leaves, minced	1	**tablespoon**
Salt	¼	**teaspoon**
Pepper		**Several grinds**

Preheat the broiler. Cut the tomatoes in half lengthwise and place cut side up on the broiler pan. Cut the onion into ¼-inch slices and arrange the slices among the tomatoes. Broil the vegetables 2 inches from the flame for about 10 minutes, or until the surfaces are well charred. Check the pan after 5 minutes and rearrange the tomatoes if they are not charring evenly. Transfer the tomatoes and onions to a plate and set aside to cool at room temperature.

When tomatoes are cool enough to handle, remove their skins and use a spoon to remove and discard the seed pockets. Combine the tomatoes and onion in a food processor with the garlic, oil, sage, salt, and pepper. Puree until homogeneous. At this point, you may store the sauce in a closed container in the refrigerator for up to a few days, or freeze it for longer periods. Just before using, place in a saucepan and simmer over medium-low heat until somewhat reduced, about 10 minutes.

Note: This recipe yields enough sauce for 12 ounces dried pasta, cooked and drained.

Each ½ cup provides:

101	Calories	16 g	Carbohydrate
3 g	Protein	160 mg	Sodium
4 g	Fat	0 mg	Cholesterol
3 g	Dietary Fiber		

Vegetable Ragout

VEGAN

A good old standby tomato sauce—easy to make and far superior to expensive jars of sauce sold at the supermarket. The recipe for this hearty, flavorful sauce yields enough to make spaghetti for a large party of friends, or you can freeze some for later use.

Yield: 10 cups

Olive oil	2	**tablespoons**
White onion	1	**large, chopped**
Garlic	4	**cloves, minced**
Green bell pepper	1	**large, diced**
Dried red chili flakes	1	**teaspoon**
Dried rosemary	1	**teaspoon**
Mushrooms	½	**pound, chopped**
Zucchini	2	**medium, grated**
Dried basil	1	**tablespoon**
Dried oregano	1	**tablespoon**
Salt	½	**teaspoon**
Whole tomatoes	1	**28-ounce can**
Tomato puree	1	**28-ounce can**
Bay leaves	2	
Red wine	½	**cup**

Heat the olive oil in a deep, heavy skillet over medium heat. Add the onion, garlic, bell pepper, chili flakes, and rosemary. Stir and sauté 5 minutes. Add the mushrooms, zucchini, basil, oregano, and salt. Stir and sauté 3 minutes. When the vegetables just begin to release their juices, add the tomatoes, tomato puree, and bay leaves. Increase the heat to medium-high and bring to a simmer. Reduce the heat to low and cook, uncovered, for 20 minutes, stirring frequently. Add the red wine and simmer an additional 10 minutes.

Note: This recipe yields enough sauce for 3½ pounds dried pasta, cooked and drained.

Each ½ cup provides:

51	Calories	8 g	Carbohydrate
1 g	Protein	272 mg	Sodium
2 g	Fat	0 mg	Cholesterol
2 g	Dietary Fiber		

Mushroom Tomato Sauce

ALMOST INSTANT, VEGAN

This easy sauce is absolutely delectable. The mushrooms are
succulent and have a wonderful roasted flavor. It will suit pasta,
polenta, or risotto.

Yield: About 2 cups

Whole pear tomatoes	**1**	**28-ounce can**
Mushrooms	**12**	**ounces**
Olive oil	**2**	**tablespoons**
Fresh Italian parsley, minced	**3**	**tablespoons**
Garlic	**2**	**cloves, minced**
Salt	**¼**	**teaspoon**
Pepper		**Several grinds**
Tomato paste	**1**	**tablespoon**

Drain the juice from the canned tomatoes and reserve it for
another use (such as soup). Chop the tomatoes coarsely into a
bowl and set aside. Brush or wipe large dirt particles from the
mushrooms and quarter them to create mushroom wedges. If
the mushrooms are nice and fresh, there is no need to discard
the stems.

Heat the olive oil over medium-high heat and stir in the
mushrooms and parsley. Stir and sauté 5 minutes, until the
mushrooms have taken on a golden hue and are beginning to

release their juices. Stir in the garlic, then add the tomatoes, salt, and pepper. Cook over medium-high heat 10–12 minutes, until the mushrooms are tender but still plump. Stir in the tomato paste and cook for another minute. Use immediately, or store in a closed container in the refrigerator for a day or two.

Note: This recipe yields enough sauce for 12 ounces dried pasta, cooked and drained.

Each serving provides:

126	Calories	14 g	Carbohydrate
3 g	Protein	484 mg	Sodium
8 g	Fat	0 mg	Cholesterol
2 g	Dietary Fiber		

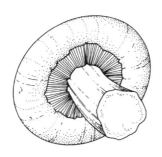

Creamy Walnut Sauce with Garlic and Parsley

ALMOST INSTANT

This sauce is popular in the Tuscany region. Our fantasia *version is sure to become one of your favorites. It is rich and creamy in flavor, with a thick pesto consistency. Thinned slightly with a tablespoon or two of hot water, it can be served over pasta or freshly steamed vegetables. As a spread for bread, simply serve it at room temperature.*

Yield: 1½ cups

Raw, unsalted walnuts, chopped	¾	**cup**
Pine nuts	¼	**cup**
Extra virgin olive oil	¼	**cup**
Parmesan cheese, finely grated	¼	**cup**
Garlic	3	**cloves, minced**
Freshly grated nutmeg	¼	**teaspoon**
Pepper		**Several grinds**
Lowfat milk	½	**cup**
Fresh Italian parsley, minced	¼	**cup**

Place the walnuts and pine nuts in a food processor. With the machine running, add the olive oil in a steady stream. The nuts will form a very thick paste. Add the Parmesan, garlic, nutmeg, pepper, and milk, and process until smooth. Add the parsley and pulse to just combine.

Note: This recipe yields enough sauce for 1¼ pounds dried pasta, cooked and drained.

Each 2 tablespoons provide:

117	Calories	3 g	Carbohydrate
3 g	Protein	38 mg	Sodium
11 g	Fat	2 mg	Cholesterol
0 g	Dietary Fiber		

Piquant Green Sauce

VEGAN

This lovely salsa verde *has the consistency and appearance of traditional basil pesto, but a much lighter taste. In Italy, it would usually include a few anchovy fillets, yet it is delicious and quite versatile without them. It is excellent as an accompaniment to roasted potatoes or grilled fish, or as a spread for crusty bread. It also makes a delicious light topping for warm pasta in the summertime, and works wonderfully in our Pizza with Salsa Verde, Roasted Peppers, and Goat Cheese (see page 288). Since the ingredients are readily available year-round, we like to keep a batch handy for quick inspiration when an impromptu dinner is in the making.*

Yield: 2 cups

Fresh Italian parsley leaves	3	**cups, lightly packed**
Extra virgin olive oil	3	**tablespoons**
Capers, drained	3	**tablespoons**
Fresh-squeezed lemon juice	2	**tablespoons**
Garlic	4	**cloves, minced**
Dried red chili flakes	¼	**teaspoon**
Salt		**A pinch**

Combine all ingredients in a food processor and puree until smooth and homogeneous. Store in a covered jar in the refrigerator for up to a week.

Note: This recipe yields enough sauce for 2 pounds dried pasta, cooked and drained.

Each ¼ cup provides:

64	Calories	4 g	Carbohydrate
1 g	Protein	106 mg	Sodium
6 g	Fat	0 mg	Cholesterol
1 g	Dietary Fiber		

Ricotta Sauce with Parsley and Garlic

ALMOST INSTANT

Most classic Italian cookbooks contain some version of this delicate yet satisfying sauce. It is extraordinary for its simplicity and its luscious creaminess. If serving over cooked pasta, use warmed dishes so the sauce doesn't stiffen too quickly. Finish the dish with toasted pine nuts and a dusting of nutmeg.

Yield: 1¾ cups

Fresh Italian parsley	1	**cup, lightly packed**
Part-skim ricotta cheese	1¼	**cups**
Italian Vegetable Stock or dry white wine	⅓	**cup**
Freshly grated Parmesan cheese	¼	**cup**
Light cream	2	**tablespoons**
Garlic	2	**cloves, minced**
Salt	½	**teaspoon**
Pepper		**Several grinds**
Cayenne pepper		**A pinch**

Remove the parsley leaves from the stems and discard the stems. Rinse the leaves well in a colander and spin dry or dry in a clean tea towel. Mince very finely, by hand or in a food processor.

In a small bowl, mix the ricotta and stock or wine until well combined, then stir in the remaining ingredients. Allow the flavors to develop at room temperature for a half hour before using the sauce. You may make it a few days ahead of time, but it should be at room temperature when used.

Note: This recipe yields enough sauce for 12 ounces dried pasta, cooked and drained.

Each ¼ cup provides:

154	Calories	6 g	Carbohydrate
12 g	Protein	480 mg	Sodium
9 g	Fat	33 mg	Cholesterol
1 g	Dietary Fiber		

Classic Cream Sauce

ALMOST INSTANT

Decidedly rich with butter and whole milk, this sauce (known in Italy as besciamella, *in France as* béchamel) *is a soul-satisfying treat stirred into hot rice, or drizzled on cooked vegetables. It can also lend its creamy richness to soups. After the basic recipe, we provide a lighter version for those who are watching their intake of fat and calories. Leftover sauce may be refrigerated for a few days and re-heated in a double boiler or briefly in a microwave oven.*

Yield: 2¼ cups

Whole milk	**2¼ cups**
Unsalted butter	**3 tablespoons**
Unbleached flour	**4 tablespoons**
Salt	**¼ teaspoon**
Pepper	**Several grinds**
Freshly grated nutmeg	**¼ teaspoon**

Heat the milk to scalding but don't allow it to boil. Keep hot. Meanwhile, melt the butter over medium heat in a heavy-bottomed saucepan. Add the flour and cook 1 minute, whisking constantly. Reduce the heat to low and add the hot milk a little at a time, stirring constantly, until it is incorporated. Continue to cook over low heat, stirring frequently to prevent scorching, until thickened—about 10 minutes. Stir in the salt, pepper, and nutmeg.

Note: For a light *besciamella,* replace the whole milk with 1 cup of lowfat milk and 1¼ cups of Italian Vegetable Stock (page 34). If you do not have homemade stock on hand, dissolve 1 low-sodium vegetable broth cube in 1¼ cups of hot water. You may use this version in any recipe calling for Classic Cream Sauce.

Each ¼ cup provides:

87	Calories	6 g	Carbohydrate
2 g	Protein	90 mg	Sodium
6 g	Fat	19 mg	Cholesterol
0 g	Dietary Fiber		

Basil Pesto

ALMOST INSTANT

We have prepared this simple version of the classic Genovese pesto for years, using aromatic basil picked fresh from our summer gardens. We enjoy pesto on pasta, as a seasoning in soups and other dishes, and as a spread on slices of bread.

Yield: 1 cup

Fresh basil leaves	2	**cups, firmly packed**
Extra virgin olive oil	⅓	**cup**
Pine nuts	¼	**cup**
Garlic	6	**cloves, chopped**
Parmesan cheese, finely grated	¾	**cup**

Wash the basil, discard the stems, and dry thoroughly. In a food processor or blender, puree the basil with ¼ cup of the olive oil, the pine nuts, garlic, and Parmesan until thick and homogeneous. With the machine running, add the remaining olive oil in a thin stream to create a smooth paste.

Note: This recipe makes enough pesto for 1½ pounds dried pasta, cooked and drained.

Each 2 tablespoons provide:

66	Calories	1 g	Carbohydrate
2 g	Protein	47 mg	Sodium
6 g	Fat	2 mg	Cholesterol
0 g	Dietary Fiber		

Sage Gorgonzola Sauce

ALMOST INSTANT

Gorgonzola elevates this simple cream sauce to great heights. Earthy sage rounds out the flavor perfectly. Serve it over polenta, gnocchi, risotto, pasta, or grilled vegetables.

Yield: 1⅔ cups

Nonfat milk	**1½**	**cups**
Unsalted butter	**2**	**tablespoons**
Unbleached flour	**2**	**tablespoons**
Dry sherry	**2**	**tablespoons**
Dried sage, crumbled	**2**	**teaspoons**
Pepper		**Several grinds**
Gorgonzola cheese, crumbled	**3**	**ounces (¾ cup)**

Heat the milk to scalding but don't allow it to boil. Keep hot. Melt the butter in a medium-size skillet over medium-low heat, then stir in the flour, sherry, sage, and pepper. Cook for about 1 minute, stirring constantly, being careful not to scorch the flour. Add the hot milk in a slow, steady stream, whisking constantly until smoothly incorporated. Cook for about 5 minutes, stirring frequently, until the sauce has thickened. Stir in the cheese and allow it to melt. If necessary, keep the sauce warm in a double boiler until you are ready to use it.

Each ¼ cup provides:

112	Calories	5 g	Carbohydrate
5 g	Protein	207 mg	Sodium
7 g	Fat	20 mg	Cholesterol
0 g	Dietary Fiber		

Garlic Maionese

ALMOST INSTANT

No store-bought mayonnaise can hold a candle to this garlic-laced homemade version. It is easy to make and keeps well. What's more, if you start from scratch you can devise mayonnaise flavors to suit your own tastes and purposes. The recipe below provides basic instructions, in addition to several ideas that will get you started on exploring possible variations. It is a wonderful topping for steamed vegetables or grilled fish, and the perfect dressing for sliced tomatoes, chilled cooked asparagus, and other simple salads. Take it easy on the portions, however, since mayonnaise is high in fat and cholesterol.

Yield: 1½ cups

Egg＊	1	**large**
Extra virgin olive oil	1	**cup**
Fresh-squeezed lemon juice＊＊	1	**tablespoon**
Red wine vinegar	1	**tablespoon**
Garlic	2	**cloves, minced**
Salt	¼	**teaspoon**
White pepper	¼	**teaspoon**

Place the egg in a blender or food processor fitted with a metal blade. Process while you quickly count to 15, then add the oil, pouring in a slow, steady stream. The egg and oil will emulsify into a thick sauce. Add the lemon juice, vinegar, garlic, salt, and pepper, and process for a few seconds to incorporate. Transfer to a glass jar and store in the refrigerator for up to 2 weeks.

＊Some authorities suggest avoiding dishes made with raw eggs, due to the remote possibility of salmonella contamination. Immune-compromised individuals may wish to heed this advice. For more information, contact your local office of the U.S. Department of Agriculture.
＊＊Be sure you use a lemon that is very ripe so its juice will not be bitter.

Tomato Maionese

Add 2 tablespoons of tomato paste or 2 reconstituted dried tomatoes, minced, to the sauce along with the lemon juice, vinegar, garlic, salt, and pepper.

Caper Maionese

Reduce the salt to ⅛ teaspoon. Rinse and drain 2 tablespoons of capers. Add them to the sauce along with the lemon juice, vinegar, garlic, salt, and pepper.

Mint Maionese

Omit the vinegar and increase the lemon juice to 2 tablespoons. Add 3 tablespoons of firmly packed, chopped fresh mint to the sauce along with the lemon juice, garlic, salt, and pepper.

Olive Maionese

Omit the salt. Add 3 tablespoons of chopped dry oil-cured black olives or green olives to the sauce along with the lemon juice, vinegar, garlic, salt, and pepper.

Each tablespoon provides:

83	Calories	0 g	Carbohydrate
0 g	Protein	25 mg	Sodium
9 g	Fat	9 mg	Cholesterol
0 g	Dietary Fiber		

Pasta

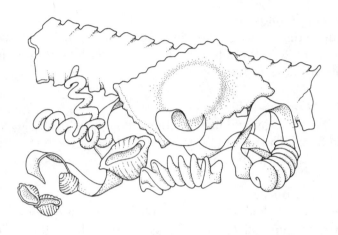

Italians love all things good to eat, and Southern Italians particularly love pasta. Over the centuries they have devised a seemingly endless variety of ways to serve it. In addition, while rice and polenta are often preferred as the starchy course in Northern Italy, some delicious pasta dishes originated in that part of the country.

Today pasta is popular around the world. It is satisfying, economical, and nutritious. In addition, most pasta dishes are quick and easy to prepare, which has earned them the favor of busy home cooks.

Every excellent pasta dish begins with excellent pasta. Italian households typically use dried pasta made in factories from semolina flour and water. Fortunately, this same type of pasta is readily available in American markets.

For stuffed pastas and some of the lighter dishes, home-made egg pasta is prepared by hand. No Italian cookbook would be complete without recipes for stuffed pasta, so we have included our favorite ravioli and cannelloni dishes. We hope you enjoy making them for special friends and family.

Tips and Tools

- Most of our recipes call for dried semolina pasta. For added fiber, you may substitute brown whole wheat pasta in any dish with a strongly seasoned sauce. Delicate sauces will not work well with the texture and taste of whole wheat pasta.

- Despite the almost universal advice of cookbooks to salt and oil the cooking water for pasta, we always get perfect results without doing either. To prevent sticking, cook pasta in plenty of water (6–8 quarts per pound of pasta) that has been brought to a strong, rolling boil. Stir the pasta vigorously a few times while it's cooking.

- Dried pasta should always be cooked to the *al dente* stage. The Italian phrase literally means "to the tooth," suggesting that the tooth should meet a little resistance when biting into the pasta. Every manufacturer provides recommended cooking times on the pasta package. Set your timer for a couple of minutes less than the recommended time, and when it goes off, remove a noodle from the pot. If it is undercooked, it will stick to your teeth when you bite into it. Continue cooking, testing again every minute or so, until the pasta is tender but not mushy. This is the sought-after al dente stage.

- Drain the al dente pasta immediately in a large, footed colander. Shake the colander to remove excess water, but do not rinse the pasta.

- If your sauce is not ready when the pasta is done, toss the cooked pasta with a drizzle of olive oil to prevent sticking, and return it to the hot pot in which it was cooked. Set aside in a warm place.

- Individual warmed plates or bowls will keep the pasta hot while you eat it.

- Ravioli can be prepared ahead of time. Once filled, they can be dusted with flour, covered with a tea towel, and held at room temperature for an hour or two before cooking. To refrigerate or freeze them for longer periods, distribute them on a baking sheet so they aren't touching. Once frozen, they can be transferred to a plastic bag.

- Since it takes less than 5 minutes to cook ravioli, don't cook them in advance. They will become tough and rubbery as they dry out.

- For removing cooked ravioli from the pot, use a skimmer, flat metal strainer, or large slotted spoon.

- The most essential investment for successful pasta is a large stockpot that holds plenty of water so the pasta can move around while it cooks. A long-handled wooden spoon is ideal for stirring the pasta.

Simple Spaghetti Sicilian Style

ALMOST INSTANT, VEGAN

The people of Sicily are so passionate about their native food that even the local bus driver will share his favorite recipe. This Sicilian pasta takes little time to prepare; it will accompany a wide variety of dishes or suffice as a light main course with a salad and bread.

Yield: 4 first-course or side-dish servings

Extra virgin olive oil	2	**tablespoons**
Garlic	3	**cloves, minced**
Dried red chili flakes	⅛	**teaspoon**
Dried spaghetti	8	**ounces**

Bring 6–8 quarts of water to a boil in a large stockpot and cook the pasta until al dente. Drain and transfer to a warm, large, shallow bowl. Meanwhile, gently heat the olive oil in a small saucepan. Add the garlic and chili flakes, and sauté for 1–2 minutes, taking care not to brown the garlic. Pour over the pasta, using a rubber spatula to get all of the oil out of the pan. Toss to coat and serve immediately.

Each serving provides:

200	Calories	28 g	Carbohydrate
5 g	Protein	1 mg	Sodium
7 g	Fat	0 mg	Cholesterol
2 g	Dietary Fiber		

Fusilli with Peas, Carrots, Garlic, and Gorgonzola

ALMOST INSTANT

This pungent pasta is a delicious indulgence. It's a great choice when time for dinner preparation is short. Use a good imported Italian Gorgonzola for the best results. Fusilli are pasta spirals, and their curves hold the sauce well; however, you can substitute a pasta with a different shape.

Yield: 4 main-course servings

Dried fusilli	10	ounces
Gorgonzola cheese, crumbled	3	ounces ($\frac{3}{4}$ cup)
Fresh-squeezed lemon juice	2	tablespoons
Olive oil	1	tablespoon
Garlic	3	cloves, minced
Salt	$\frac{1}{8}$	teaspoon
Pepper		Several grinds
Carrot	1	large, diced small
Peas, fresh or frozen	8	ounces
Green onions, minced	2	
Lemon wedges	1	per person

Bring several quarts of water to a boil. Cook the pasta until al dente, adding the diced carrot for the final 3 minutes of cooking time, and the peas for the final 2 minutes if fresh or 1 minute if frozen.

Meanwhile, mash together the cheese, lemon juice, oil, garlic, salt, and pepper in a bowl until somewhat creamy but not smooth.

Before draining the pasta, add ¼ cup of the pasta-cooking water to the cheese mixture and stir to combine. Drain the pasta and vegetables, and immediately combine in a warmed serving bowl with the cheese mixture and green onions. Toss until the cheese begins to melt, creating a light sauce. Serve very hot, on warmed plates. Pass the pepper grinder and wedges of lemon.

Each serving provides:

436	Calories	67 g	Carbohydrate
17 g	Protein	428 mg	Sodium
11 g	Fat	16 mg	Cholesterol
4 g	Dietary Fiber		

Spaghetti alla Carbonara with Dried Tomato

ALMOST INSTANT

In Italy, this dish is typically made with pancetta, a smoky Italian bacon. Here we use browned onions and dried tomatoes for an equally flavorful meatless version. It is essential to add the pasta while it is steaming hot to the egg mixture so the eggs will cook a little. Be sure to have everything else ready at the moment you drain the pasta.

Yield: 4 main-course servings

Dried tomatoes	1	cup
Dry sherry	½	cup
Dried spaghetti	12	ounces
Olive oil	1	tablespoon
White onion	1	medium, chopped
Garlic	2	cloves, minced
Fresh Italian parsley, minced	⅓	cup
Salt	¼	teaspoon
Eggs*	2	large
Parmesan cheese, finely grated	⅓	cup
Dried red chili flakes	¼	teaspoon

Bring several quarts of water to a boil for the pasta. Meanwhile, place the dried tomatoes in a saucepan with the sherry and cook, covered, over very low heat for about 7 minutes, until tomatoes

*Some authorities suggest avoiding dishes made with raw eggs, due to the remote possibility of salmonella contamination. Immune-compromised individuals may wish to heed this advice. For more information, contact your local office of the U.S. Department of Agriculture.

are plump, tender, and juicy. Transfer to a bowl and allow to cool. When cool enough to handle, remove the dried tomatoes from the sherry and chop into roughly ½-inch pieces. Set the tomatoes and sherry aside separately.

Heat the olive oil over medium heat. Add the onion and garlic, and sauté about 7 minutes, stirring frequently, until the onion is nicely browned. Meanwhile, beat the eggs with the cheese and chili flakes in a large, shallow, warmed serving bowl (if the bowl is cold to the touch, run hot water over it to take off the chill). Set aside.

When onion is done, stir in the tomatoes, salt, and parsley, then pour in the sherry and immediately cover the pan. Turn off the heat.

Meanwhile, cook the spaghetti until al dente, drain briefly, and transfer at once to the bowl containing the egg mixture. Toss quickly. The pasta must be steaming hot at this point so the egg cooks slightly. Immediately add the onion mixture, using a rubber spatula to scrape all the browned bits out of the pan. Toss for a moment or two, until the cheese melts and the pasta is coated with the creamy sauce. Serve in warmed serving bowls, passing additional Parmesan and pepper, if you wish.

Each serving provides:

504	Calories	78 g	Carbohydrate
20 g	Protein	582 mg	Sodium
10 g	Fat	112 mg	Cholesterol
3 g	Dietary Fiber		

Bucatini with Green Beans, Tomatoes, and Olives

VEGAN

Bucatini are hollow strands of pasta with a distinctive texture. If you are unable to locate them at an Italian specialty food store, you may substitute another hearty pasta variety, such as rigatoni or fusilli. This dish is robust, wholesome, and delicious.

Yield: 4 main-course servings

Fresh green beans	¾	**pound**
Whole tomatoes	1	**28-ounce can**
Olive oil	1	**tablespoon**
Garlic	2	**cloves, minced**
Dried red chili flakes	⅛	**teaspoon**
Salt	⅛	**teaspoon**
Port	¼	**cup**
Ground cloves		**A pinch**
Tomato paste	1	**tablespoon**
Dry oil-cured black olives, pitted and minced	2	**tablespoons**
Dried bucatini	¾	**pound**

Snap off the ends of the beans and pull off any strings. Cut the beans crosswise at a slant into 1-inch lengths. Drain the tomatoes, saving their juice for another use. Coarsely chop the tomatoes and set aside in a bowl.

Heat the olive oil over medium heat in a large skillet and sauté the garlic and chili flakes for about 1 minute, then add the beans and salt. Sauté, stirring frequently, for 3–4 minutes, then add the tomatoes, port, and cloves. Reduce heat to low, cover, and cook 15–20 minutes, until beans are fork-tender. Turn off the heat and stir in the tomato paste and olives.

Meanwhile, bring several quarts of water to a boil and cook the pasta until al dente. Drain well, add to the skillet, and toss with the hot sauce. Serve immediately.

Each serving provides:

444	Calories	80 g	Carbohydrate
14 g	Protein	457 mg	Sodium
7 g	Fat	0 mg	Cholesterol
5 g	Dietary Fiber		

Pasta with Fresh Fava Beans, Tomatoes, Rosemary, and Gorgonzola

Fava beans have become a nutritious, tasty, and unusual addition to our spring vegetable repertoire. In this recipe, the shelled beans are cooked with tomatoes, rosemary, and garlic, and served with pasta— quite appropriate to their Sicilian heritage. The Gorgonzola adds a rich, piquant note.

Yield: 4 main-course servings

Fava beans, in their pods	**1¼**	**pounds**
Fresh pear tomatoes	**1¼**	**pounds**
Olive oil	**2**	**tablespoons**
Yellow onion	**1**	**small, diced**
Garlic	**4**	**cloves, minced**
Fresh rosemary leaves, minced	**1**	**tablespoon**
Dried red chili flakes	**⅛**	**teaspoon**
Dry white wine	**⅓**	**cup**
Salt	**¼**	**teaspoon**
Dried penne	**12**	**ounces**
Gorgonzola cheese, crumbled	**2**	**ounces (½ cup)**

In a stockpot, bring several quarts of water to a boil. Shell the fava beans and plunge them into the boiling water for 2 minutes. Remove with a slotted spoon and cool them under cold running water. Peel the beans and set aside. Return the water to a boil. (If the beans are small and just picked from the garden, there may be no need to blanch and peel them.)

Blanch, peel, and seed the tomatoes according to the directions on page 27. Chop them coarsely into a bowl. Bring the water back to a boil for the pasta.

Heat 1 tablespoon of the olive oil in a heavy-bottomed skillet over medium-high heat and sauté the onion, garlic, rosemary, and chili flakes for 5 minutes. Add the tomatoes, white wine, and salt, and bring to a simmer. Reduce the heat to medium-low, cover, and cook for 8 minutes. Add the favas and cook an additional 2–5 minutes, until the beans are fork-tender.

Meanwhile, cook the pasta in the boiling water until al dente and drain well. Toss the pasta with the remaining tablespoon of olive oil and the Gorgonzola in a warmed serving bowl, then toss again with the tomato sauce. Serve immediately.

Each serving provides:

559	Calories	87 g	Carbohydrate
21 g	Protein	411 mg	Sodium
13 g	Fat	13 mg	Cholesterol
8 g	Dietary Fiber		

Fettuccine with Zucchini, Roasted Peppers, Almonds, and Mint

ALMOST INSTANT, VEGAN

This has become a standby in our kitchens. It is made from easy-to-find ingredients and comes together quickly. Select firm, small zucchini; they will have the best flavor and texture. You may wish to roast the peppers and toast the almonds earlier in the day to save yourself the effort at mealtime.

Yield: 4 main-course servings

Red bell peppers	2	large
Slivered almonds	¼	cup
Zucchini	1	pound (3 medium)
White onion	1	medium
Olive oil	3	tablespoons
Garlic	4	cloves, minced
Dried red chili flakes	¼	teaspoon
Salt	¼	teaspoon
Fresh mint leaves, minced	¾	cup
Dry white wine	½	cup
Fresh-squeezed lemon juice	3	tablespoons
Dried fettuccine	10	ounces

Roast the peppers (see page 29). Peel them, discarding stems, seeds, and white membrane, and cut into thin 1-inch-long pieces. Set aside. Toast the almonds (see page 31) and set aside. Wash and dry the zucchini, then cut into ¼-inch rounds. Trim off and discard the ends of the onion, peel it, and cut it in half lengthwise. Place each half cut side down on your work surface and slice lengthwise into ¼-inch-thick slices.

In a large pot, bring a few quarts of water to a boil for the pasta. Meanwhile, heat the oil in a large skillet over medium heat. Sauté the onion, garlic, and chili flakes for about 5 minutes, until the onion begins to turn golden. Add the zucchini and salt, then sauté about 15 minutes over medium-high heat, stirring frequently. The vegetables should be nicely browned. Stir in the mint and bell pepper strips, then add the wine and lemon juice. Stir and sauté about 1 minute. Cover the pan, turn off the heat, and allow to sit 5–15 minutes.

Meanwhile, cook the pasta in the boiling water until al dente and drain well. Toss the pasta with the zucchini mixture and almonds until well combined.

Each serving provides:

469	Calories	68 g	Carbohydrate
13 g	Protein	149 mg	Sodium
15 g	Fat	0 mg	Cholesterol
6 g	Dietary Fiber		

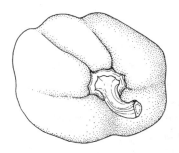

Pasta with Stewed Tomatoes, Cauliflower, and Red Wine

Hearty and robust, this pasta makes an appetizing first course for 8; as a main dish, served with an antipasto and salad, it will satisfy 6. This dish will make you feel as if you are sitting around the kitchen table in a home in the Italian countryside.

Yield: 6 main-course servings

Olive oil	1	tablespoon
Garlic	2	cloves, minced
Yellow onion	1	medium, diced
Fresh rosemary, minced	1	teaspoon
Whole pear tomatoes	1	28-ounce can
Cauliflower	4	cups, chopped
Red wine	¼	cup
Dry oil-cured black olives, minced	¼	cup
Dried fusilli	16	ounces
Asiago cheese, coarsely grated	2	ounces (about 1 cup)

Heat the oil over medium heat in a large pan that has a tight-fitting lid. Add the garlic, onion, and rosemary, and sauté for 5 minutes, stirring frequently. Drain the liquid from the tomatoes into the pan; chop the tomatoes and add them along with the cauliflower. Pour in the wine, stir to combine, cover, and cook 25 minutes over medium-high heat.

Meanwhile, bring several quarts of water to a boil in a large stockpot. Cook the pasta until al dente. Drain well and transfer to a warmed large bowl.

When the cauliflower is fork-tender, stir in the olives and continue to cook, uncovered, for 5 minutes. The resulting sauce should be thick and chunky. Pour it over the hot pasta and toss to combine. Sprinkle with the cheese, toss again and serve immediately, passing additional cheese if desired.

Each serving provides:

416	Calories	70 g	Carbohydrate
15 g	Protein	479 mg	Sodium
8 g	Fat	10 mg	Cholesterol
5 g	Dietary Fiber		

Farfalle with Artichoke Pesto and Mascarpone

Pesto *can take many forms. This recipe creates a slightly tart yet creamy pesto sauce for pasta, or a delicious spread for bread. This is an excellent way to use the leaves trimmed off when preparing artichoke hearts for another recipe, such as Artichokes Braised with Parsley and Lemon (page 250). Simply steam the leaves and scrape them with a spoon to remove the tender, edible pulp. Alternately, you may use the pureed bottom of a cooked artichoke as the pulp called for below. If you are unable to locate mascarpone cheese, you may substitute an equal amount of cream cheese and ½ teaspoon of sugar for different (but good) results.* Farfalle *have a bow-tie shape. You can also use rigatoni.*

Yield: 6 first-course or side-dish servings

Artichoke pulp	⅓	**cup**
Extra virgin olive oil	3	**tablespoons**
Fresh-squeezed lemon juice	2	**tablespoons**
Parmesan cheese, finely grated	¼	**cup**
Fresh Italian parsley, chopped	¼	**cup**
Mascarpone cheese	2	**tablespoons**
Dried farfalle or rigatoni	12	**ounces**

Bring several quarts of water to a boil in a large stockpot and cook the pasta until al dente. Drain and place in a warmed serving bowl. Reserve 2 tablespoons of the pasta-cooking water for the sauce.

Meanwhile, place the artichoke pulp in a food processor. With the machine running, add the olive oil and lemon juice in a slow, steady stream. Add the Parmesan and pulse to incorporate. Add the parsley and mascarpone; pulse just enough to combine. Mix the reserved two tablespoons of pasta-cooking water into the pesto to thin it slightly, then toss with the hot cooked pasta. Serve immediately.

Each serving provides:

318	Calories	46 g	Carbohydrate
9 g	Protein	74 mg	Sodium
11 g	Fat	10 mg	Cholesterol
2 g	Dietary Fiber		

Fusilli in Mascarpone Sauce with Grilled Peppers and Portobello Mushrooms

Pasta is the perfect medium for showcasing grilled vegetables. This recipe pairs pasta with grilled mushrooms and sweet red peppers. Portobello mushrooms have a full, woodsy flavor. They are imported from Italy as well as cultivated in the United States. Fusilli pasta is a short or long corkscrew-shaped noodle that holds the sauce well. Seek out the ingredients that are unfamiliar to you; most major grocery stores carry them, or visit your local Italian market.

Yield: 6 main-course servings

Olive oil	¼	cup
Fresh-squeezed lemon juice	2	tablespoons
Fresh Italian parsley, minced	1	tablespoon
Garlic	3	cloves, minced
Salt		A pinch
Pepper		Several grinds
Fresh portobello mushrooms	8	ounces
Red bell pepper	1	large
Dried fusilli	12	ounces
Italian Vegetable Stock*	1¼	cups
Dried oregano	1	teaspoon
Unbleached flour	1	tablespoon
Mascarpone cheese	2	tablespoons

*If you do not have Italian Vegetable Stock on hand, make some according to the directions on page 34, or dissolve ½ of a large, low-sodium vegetable broth cube in 1¼ cups of hot water.

Preheat a coal or gas grill to medium high (see page 29).

Whisk together the oil, lemon juice, parsley, 1 clove of garlic, salt, and pepper in a bowl. Cut the mushrooms into ½-inch slices, place them on a shallow platter, and pour the oil mixture over them. Turn to coat the other side and allow to marinate for 15 minutes. Meanwhile, cut the bell pepper in half, discard the stem, seeds, and pithy membranes, then slice each half in thirds lengthwise. Place the peppers on a fine-mesh grilling rack on the grill, cover the grill, and cook 12–15 minutes, turning several times while they are cooking. They will char slightly and become limp. Transfer from the grill to a plate, and set aside in a warm place. Put the mushrooms on the grill for 5–7 minutes. They should char slightly but not burn. Remove from the grill and place them on the plate with the peppers. When cool enough to handle, coarsely chop the peppers and mushrooms, and set aside in a warm place.

Meanwhile, bring a large pot of water to a boil and cook the pasta until al dente. While the pasta is cooking, pour the stock into a small skillet over medium-high heat. Add the remaining 2 cloves of garlic and the oregano, and simmer for 5 minutes. Place 2 tablespoons of cold water in a small jar that has a tight-fitting lid and add the flour. Put the lid on and shake vigorously to dissolve the flour. Spoon in a couple of tablespoons of the hot stock and shake again. Whisk this into the hot stock, stirring as it thickens. Add the mascarpone, stirring to incorporate. The sauce will be smooth and fairly thin.

Drain the pasta well and toss with the sauce. Add the mushrooms and peppers, and toss again. Serve immediately.

Each serving provides:

294	Calories	53 g	Carbohydrate
9 g	Protein	70 mg	Sodium
5 g	Fat	7 mg	Cholesterol
2 g	Dietary Fiber		

Fettuccine Alfredo

ALMOST INSTANT

Legend has it that fettuccine Alfredo originated in a small restaurant in Rome, where Alfredo prepared it for his pregnant wife. The creation resulted in the birth of a great sauce and a son, Alfredo II. Our version uses half-and-half in place of the traditional heavy cream and much less butter. We enjoy it as a side dish, though it can become a main dish for 4 when accompanied with bread, salad, and a steamed vegetable.

Yield: 6 first-course or side-dish servings

Dried fettuccine	12	ounces
Half-and-half	2	cups
Unsalted butter	2	tablespoons
Garlic	3	cloves, minced
Freshly grated nutmeg	½	teaspoon
Salt	¼	teaspoon
Pepper		Several grinds
Egg yolk°	1	large, lightly beaten
Parmesan cheese, finely grated	1	cup

Bring several quarts of water to a boil and cook the pasta until al dente.

Meanwhile, warm the half-and-half in a small saucepan over very low heat. Melt the butter in a deep skillet over low heat and sauté the garlic for about 3 minutes. Whisk in the warm half-and-half, nutmeg, salt, and pepper. Continue to cook over

°Some authorities suggest avoiding dishes made with raw eggs, due to the remote possibility of salmonella contamination. Immune-compromised individuals may wish to heed this advice. For more information, contact your local office of the U.S. Department of Agriculture.

medium-low heat for about 15 minutes until the sauce begins to simmer, stirring occasionally.

As soon as the sauce starts to bubble, add the hot cooked pasta and remove the pan from the heat. Push the noodles toward the sides of the pan to create a "well" in the center. Pour the beaten egg into this well and—very quickly but carefully—begin to lift and toss the pasta with the sauce until the egg is smoothly incorporated. The heat of the sauce and pasta will cook the egg slightly to create a thick, creamy sauce that clings to the noodles. Add the Parmesan and continue lifting and tossing until it is smoothly incorporated. If the pasta seems more gooey than creamy, drizzle on some hot water and toss again until the right consistency is achieved. Serve immediately on warmed plates, passing additional Parmesan and pepper, if desired.

Each serving provides:

371	Calories	48 g	Carbohydrate
10 g	Protein	126 mg	Sodium
15 g	Fat	74 mg	Cholesterol
2 g	Dietary Fiber		

Pasta with Lentils, Fresh Sage, and Ricotta Cheese

Hearty and delicious, this combination of earthy flavors will satisfy big appetites. More chili flakes may be added if you are in a spicy mood.

Yield: 4 main-course servings

Dried brown lentils	¾	**cup**
Olive oil	1	**tablespoon**
Dried red chili flakes	¼	**teaspoon**
Garlic	4	**cloves, minced**
Yellow onion	1	**medium, diced**
Celery	1	**rib, thinly sliced**
Dried thyme	¼	**teaspoon**
Dry white wine	⅓	**cup**
Salt	¼	**teaspoon plus ⅛ teaspoon**
Fresh sage leaves, slivered	⅓	**cup**
Dried linguine	10	**ounces**
Part-skim ricotta cheese	1	**cup**

Sort through the lentils, discarding any small pebbles you find. Rinse the lentils and set aside.

In a large skillet or sauté pan, heat the olive oil over medium heat. Add the chili flakes and garlic, and stir briefly, then add the onion, celery, and thyme. Stir and sauté 5 minutes, then add the lentils, wine, 1½ cups of water, and ¼ teaspoon of the salt. Cover, reduce heat to medium-low, and simmer about 25–30 minutes, until lentils are tender but not falling apart. Stir in the sage, replace the lid, and turn off the heat.

Meanwhile, bring several quarts of water to a boil in a stockpot and cook the pasta until al dente. Before draining the pasta, remove ¾ cup of cooking water. Add the drained pasta to the lentil sauce in the skillet. In a small bowl, stir the reserved cooking liquid into the ricotta cheese, along with the remaining ⅛ teaspoon of salt, until well combined. The resulting mixture will be thin.

In a warmed serving bowl, combine the hot pasta and lentil sauce with the ricotta mixture until well distributed. Serve immediately.

Each serving provides:

540	Calories	84 g	Carbohydrate
27 g	Protein	254 mg	Sodium
10 g	Fat	19 mg	Cholesterol
7 g	Dietary Fiber		

Baked Pasta with Tomato Nutmeg Sauce

This dish can be made in a lasagna pan, but the presentation is especially wonderful when baked in individual au gratin dishes. The mafalda pasta called for in this recipe has fluted edges and resembles narrow lasagna noodles. If it is not available, use the slightly narrower lasagnette noodles. This recipe can be prepared ahead of time, making it ideal to serve at a dinner party.

Yield: 6 main-course servings

Mafalda pasta	1	**pound**
Part-skim ricotta cheese	15	**ounces**
Fresh basil leaves, minced	½	**cup**
Part-skim mozzarella cheese, grated	6	**ounces (1½ cups)**
Pear tomatoes	3	**28-ounce cans**
Olive oil	2	**tablespoons plus ¼ teaspoon**
Marsala wine	¼	**cup**
Garlic	3	**cloves, minced**
Freshly grated nutmeg	¾	**teaspoon**

Drain the tomatoes (reserving the canning juice for another use) and coarsely chop them in a large bowl to catch the resulting juices. Heat 2 tablespoons of olive oil and Marsala in a large skillet over medium heat and add the garlic. Sauté for 2 minutes, add the juicy chopped tomatoes, and then the nutmeg. Cook over medium-high heat for 40 minutes, stirring occasionally. The liquid will reduce so the sauce becomes thick and chunky.

Meanwhile, bring several quarts of water to a boil in a large stockpot and cook the noodles until just al dente. Combine the ricotta and basil in a bowl while the noodles are cooking. Drain the noodles well in a colander. Preheat the oven to 350 degrees F.

Rub the bottoms of 6 individual au gratin dishes, or a 9 × 13-inch glass baking dish, with the remaining ¼ teaspoon of oil. Spread ⅓ of the noodles in a single layer on the bottoms of the individual dishes, or the casserole dish, top with the ricotta mixture, layer on another ⅓ of the noodles, add the mozzarella cheese, then top with the remaining noodles. Spoon the sauce evenly over the top. Cover and bake 20–25 minutes. Serve immediately.

Each serving provides:

556	Calories	74 g	Carbohydrate
27 g	Protein	701 mg	Sodium
17 g	Fat	37 mg	Cholesterol
3 g	Dietary Fiber		

Pasta Shells Stuffed with Spinach, Ricotta, and Mozzarella

This is a wonderful dish to make for family gatherings because it can be prepared ahead of time and because both children and adults will enjoy it. Serve it with a green salad, Grilled Italian Garlic Bread (page 40), and a light red wine.

Yield: 8 main-course servings

Dried jumbo pasta shells	12	**ounces**
Fresh Tomato Coulis	4	**cups**
Fresh spinach		
(or 1 10-ounce package		
frozen)	1	**pound**
Part-skim ricotta cheese	2	**cups**
Part-skim mozzarella, grated	2	**ounces (½ cup)**
Freshly grated nutmeg	¼	**teaspoon**
Salt	⅛	**teaspoon**
Pepper		**Several grinds**

Bring several quarts of water to a boil in a large stockpot. Cook the pasta until almost al dente, about 9 minutes. It will finish cooking in the oven. Carefully transfer the shells to a colander to drain, then place them on a tea towel to dry. Preheat the oven to 350 degrees F.

Meanwhile, prepare a double batch of the Fresh Tomato Coulis according to the directions on page 114, using thyme and rosemary as the seasonings. Set aside on the stove.

Remove and discard the stems of the spinach and place the leaves in a large basin of cold water. Gently but thoroughly agitate the leaves, then allow them to sit in the basin for several minutes while the dirt sinks to the bottom. Carefully lift out the spinach and place it in a colander. Rinse well. Pile it into a large pan, allowing the water to cling to the leaves. Cover and heat over medium until the leaves wilt, about 5 minutes. Drain well in a colander, pressing with the back of a spoon to remove as much moisture as possible. Coarsely chop the spinach and combine it in a bowl with the ricotta, mozzarella, nutmeg, salt, and pepper.

Spoon three-fourths of the coulis over the bottom of a 9 × 13-inch casserole dish. One at a time, carefully fill the shells with the ricotta mixture and place them on top of the sauce in the pan. Drizzle with the remaining sauce, cover, and bake for 30 minutes. Serve immediately.

Each serving provides:

354	Calories	48 g	Carbohydrate
18 g	Protein	501 mg	Sodium
11 g	Fat	23 mg	Cholesterol
6 g	Dietary Fiber		

Spinach and Grilled
Eggplant Lasagna

The lightness of this fantasia lasagna is reminiscent of foods native to Campania and Sicily, where eggplants grow in abundance, as do tomatoes and basil. These regions are also noted for their pasta and for rustic meals. This lasagna takes about 1½ hours to prepare, but it is well worth the time. Add it to your repertoire of "do ahead" dinner party main dishes.

Yield: 10 main-course servings

Dried lasagna noodles	12	ounces

The sauce

Olive oil	1	tablespoon
Garlic	2	cloves, minced
Yellow onion	1	medium, diced
Stewed tomatoes	1	28-ounce can
Fresh lemon	2	slices
Bay leaves	3	
Pepper		Several grinds
Fresh basil leaves, minced	3	tablespoons

The filling

Fresh spinach	¾	pound (1 bunch)
Eggplant	1	pound (1 medium)
Olive oil	3	tablespoons plus ¼ teaspoon

Part-skim ricotta cheese	2½	cups
		(20 ounces)
Garlic	3	cloves, minced
Part-skim mozzarella cheese, grated	12	ounces (3 cups)
Parmesan cheese, finely grated	⅓	cup

Preheat the oven to 350 degrees F. about 30 minutes before you are ready to bake the lasagna.

In a stockpot, bring several quarts of water to a boil and cook the noodles until almost al dente, 10–12 minutes. They will finish cooking in the oven. Fill a large bowl with cold water and add 1 teaspoon of the olive oil. Drain the noodles in a colander, then plunge them into the water to cool. Drain again and carefully place them on a tea towel to dry.

Meanwhile, prepare the sauce by heating 1 tablespoon of olive oil in a large pan over medium-low heat. Add the garlic and onion, and sauté for 2–3 minutes. Add the tomatoes, lemon slices, bay leaves, and pepper. Increase heat to medium-high and cook 25–30 minutes, stirring occasionally, until sauce reduces slightly. Add the fresh basil during the last 10 minutes of cooking time. Remove from the heat and discard the bay leaves and lemon slices.

While the sauce is cooking, remove and discard the stems from the spinach and place the leaves in a large basin of cold water. Gently but thoroughly agitate the leaves, then allow them to sit in the basin for several minutes while the dirt sinks to the bottom. Carefully lift out the spinach and place in a colander. Rinse well. Pile it into a large pan, allowing the water to cling to the leaves. Cover and heat over medium until the leaves wilt, about 5 minutes. Drain well in a colander, pressing with the back of a spoon to remove as much moisture as possible. Coarsely chop the spinach and set it aside.

Preheat the broiler or prepare a coal or gas grill to medium-high. Without peeling, cut the eggplant lengthwise into ½-inch-thick slices. Use 1 tablespoon of the oil to brush one side of the eggplant slices. Place them on the grill oiled side down, or under the broiler oiled side up. Cook for about 5 minutes, until slightly charred. Brush the other side with 1 tablespoon of oil, then turn and continue to cook until charred and soft, about 5 minutes longer. Carefully remove to a platter.

In a bowl, combine the ricotta cheese and garlic. Rub an 11 × 14-inch baking dish with the remaining ¼ teaspoon of olive oil. Layer the lasagna as follows:

Half the tomato sauce

One-third of the noodles

All the eggplant slices

Half of the mozzarella cheese

One-third of the noodles

Remaining tomato sauce

All of the ricotta mixture

All of the spinach

Remaining one-third of the noodles

Remaining mozzarella

All of the Parmesan

Cover and bake 30–40 minutes, until the sauce bubbles in the pan. Let stand 15 minutes before serving.

Each serving provides:

407	Calories	40 g	Carbohydrate
23 g	Protein	518 mg	Sodium
19 g	Fat	41 mg	Cholesterol
3 g	Dietary Fiber		

Fresh Homemade Pasta

*The simplest homemade pasta, made with only flour and eggs, may
also be the best. Try it some afternoon when you are in the mood to
spend a few hours in the kitchen preparing a truly special meal for
family and friends. This recipe provides instructions for making pasta
with a standard metal hand-cranked pasta machine that rolls out the
dough evenly, then cuts it into ribbons with the aid of a special
attachment. These machines are great time-savers and worth the
investment. Alternately, you may try rolling the dough out with a
long rolling pin on a very large floured surface, but you must work
quickly to finish before the dough begins to dry out.*

Yield: 4 main-course servings

Unbleached flour	**2–2¼**	**cups**
Eggs	**2**	**large**

For green pasta
Cooked spinach (frozen is fine), finely chopped	**2**	**tablespoons**

Make a mound of the flour on a clean, preferably wooden, work
surface. Use your hands to make a well in the center of the
mound. The well will be surrounded by flour walls. Break the
eggs into this well. Use a fork to beat the eggs lightly until well
broken. If you want to make a green pasta, beat the minced
spinach into the eggs. Now begin to incorporate the flour into
the eggs little by little, using the fork to take a small amount at
a time from the inner surface of the walls of the well. Use your
free hand to shore up the outer wall surface of the well. You
must work slowly and patiently—if you break the wall of the
well, the eggs will flow out onto your work surface.

When the eggs have incorporated enough dough to hold
together like a very soft paste, use your hands or a pastry scraper

to push most of the remaining flour to the side of your work surface. Now use a pastry scraper or your hands to begin folding in larger amounts of flour. Sprinkle a handful of flour over the dough and turn the dough over loosely to incorporate the flour. Continue until you have a dough that holds together well and is suitable for kneading, though it should still be quite sticky.

Clean the sticky bits of dough from your work surface with the scraper or a metal spatula, then dust the surface liberally with flour. Place the dough on the floured board and begin kneading it by folding it in half toward you, then pushing it away from you with the palm of one hand, pressing gently against the board and pivoting the dough a quarter turn after each kneading stroke. Dust the dough with more flour, 1 tablespoon at a time, if the dough continues to stick to the board and to your hands. As you proceed with the kneading, add as much flour as necessary, about 1 tablespoon at a time, until you have a soft, smooth, pliable ball of dough that does not stick to the work surface. Don't try to hurry the process by adding too much flour at one time, since this can ruin the texture of the noodle.

After 7–8 minutes of kneading, the dough should be ready. One test is to poke a hole in the dough with your finger. If your finger emerges only barely sticky and the dough bounces back quickly to close the hole, it is ready. Cover the dough with a clean towel and set it aside to rest for at least 15 minutes or as long as a few hours. Resting softens the gluten in the flour and makes the dough easier to roll out.

Meanwhile, clean the work surface again with the scraper and dust with flour. Set up your pasta rolling machine nearby. After dough has rested, cut off an oblong piece about the size of the palm of your hand. With your hands, flatten the small piece of dough so it is a neat oval about ½ inch thick. Set the pasta rolling machine to the widest setting and crank the oval of dough through the rollers. Fold the resulting dough in half lengthwise and pass through the machine 4 or 5 more times, folding in half lengthwise each time. If the dough sticks to the machine at any point in the rolling process, dust it with a small amount of flour and continue.

Adjust the machine to the next (thinner) setting and run the pasta through once. Adjust the rollers down successively, running the pasta through once on each setting until you have run it through the next-to-thinnest setting. You will have a very long, thin sheet of dough a few inches wide.

For ribbons or strands: Roll out all the dough as described above. Dust each sheet liberally with flour and stack the sheets loosely. Allow the sheets of dough to dry for 20–30 minutes before rolling each sheet into a soft, loose roll and cutting into desired widths with a sharp knife (or cut the dough using the cutting attachment of your pasta machine). Once the pasta is cut into ribbons, dust them with a little more flour and set them aside until cooking time in a loose pile on the work surface.

For ravioli: Work with one sheet of pasta at a time, immediately after rolling it out. You do not want the dough to dry before it is stuffed. Lay the sheet of dough on a clean, flat, lightly floured work surface. Cut the sheet in half lengthwise. Dot one half with filling, using 1 heaping teaspoon of filling for each ravioli, forming the filling into a mound, and spacing the mounds about 2 inches apart on the dough. The pasta half-sheet should be wide enough to accommodate two rows of mounds. Moisten your finger with water and "paint" stripes of water on the dough along all the edges and between the rows of filling. Lay the other half of the pasta sheet over the half-sheet with the filling, then stretch it very gently so that the edges meet. With your fingers, press around each mound to expel any trapped air as you begin to seal the two sheets of dough together around the filling. Cut the ravioli apart with a fluted pastry wheel, which will seal the ravioli as it cuts, or cut them apart with a sharp knife and press around the edges of each one with a fork to seal tightly. Be sure all the ravioli are well sealed. Set the filled ravioli aside on a lightly floured surface; don't allow them to touch or they will stick together. Cover with a dry towel while you roll out the remaining dough and fill it to create ravioli.

For cannelloni: Cut the sheets of pasta into rectangles 5 inches wide and about 9 inches long. Meanwhile, bring several quarts of water to a boil in a large stockpot. Fill a large bowl with cold water and place it in a handy spot near the boiling pot. Lay out a few clean, dry towels on the work surface. Drop the pasta sheets into the boiling water 2 at a time, cooking only 30 seconds. Remove the sheets with a skimmer or slotted spoon, plunge them briefly into the cold water, drain well, and lay out to dry on the towels. Proceed until you have precooked all the pasta sheets. Spread the pasta sheets with a thin layer of your preferred filling and roll up jelly-roll fashion; place the rolls seam side down in a baking pan and cover with sauce. They are ready for baking.

Each serving provides:

265	Calories	48 g	Carbohydrate
10 g	Protein	32 mg	Sodium
3 g	Fat	106 mg	Cholesterol
2 g	Dietary Fiber		

Pasta

Mushroom Ravioli with
Basil Shallot Cream Sauce

This is a wonderful dish for company. When the mushrooms for the filling are cooked, they create an intensely earthy flavor, which is perfectly complemented by the light basil cream sauce. You may purchase a 1-pound package of fresh wonton wrappers instead of making homemade pasta, if you wish.

Yield: 6 main-course servings

The filling

Olive oil	1½	**tablespoons**
Yellow onion	1	**medium**
Fresh parsley leaves, minced	¼	**cup**
Garlic	2	**cloves, minced**
Day-old bread	1½	**ounces**
Dry white wine	3	**tablespoons**
Button mushrooms	¾	**pound**
Salt	½	**teaspoon**
Pepper		**Several grinds**

The pasta

Fresh Homemade Pasta (or 1 pound fresh wonton wrappers)	1	**recipe**

The sauce

Unsalted butter	2	**tablespoons**
Shallots, peeled and minced	4	**medium**
Italian Vegetable Stock	1	**cup**
Fresh basil leaves, slivered	½	**cup**
Heavy cream	¼	**cup**
Salt	⅛	**teaspoon**
Parmesan cheese, finely grated	⅓	**cup**

To make the filling, heat the olive oil over medium heat and sauté the onion and parsley for 5 minutes, stirring occasionally. Meanwhile, wipe any obvious dirt from the mushrooms. Mince the garlic briefly in a food processor, then add the mushrooms and pulse to finely mince them. Be careful not to puree them by overprocessing. (You may, of course, mince the garlic and mushrooms by hand.)

When onions are golden and translucent, add the minced mushrooms, salt, and pepper. Sauté about 10 minutes, stirring often, until the mushrooms have released their liquid and most of it has evaporated. Meanwhile, tear the bread into large pieces and place in the food processor. Pulse to achieve a coarse crumb consistency, then combine in a bowl with the cooked mushroom mixture and wine. (Alternately, tear the bread into tiny bits with your hands before combining with the other ingredients.) Set this filling aside at room temperature.

If you want to use homemade pasta, prepare the Fresh Homemade Pasta and fill the ravioli according to the directions on page 171.

---

*If you do not have Italian Vegetable Stock on hand, make up a batch according to the directions on page 34, or dissolve ½ large low-sodium vegetable broth cube in 1 cup of hot water.

Otherwise, use a 1-pound package of fresh wonton wrappers from the supermarket. Lay several wrappers side by side on a lightly floured work surface. Place a heaping teaspoon of filling at the center of each, moisten the edges with water, and top each one with another wrapper. Press all around the filling with your fingers, expelling any trapped air, then press around the edge of each ravioli with a fork to completely seal in the filling. Set the filled ravioli aside on a lightly floured surface; don't allow them to touch or they will stick together. Cover with a dry towel while you fill the remaining ravioli. Proceed until you have used all the filling. (You may keep them on the counter for an hour or so at this point. Instructions for refrigerating or freezing ravioli are given in the Tips and Tools section at the beginning of the chapter on page 140.)

Meanwhile, bring several quarts of water to a rapid boil. But before cooking the ravioli, begin the sauce. In a large skillet or sauté pan, melt the butter over medium heat. Before it begins to brown, add the shallots and stir for a moment, then add the stock and bring to a boil over medium-high heat. Simmer rapidly about 5 minutes or until the volume is reduced by half. Add the basil, cream, and salt, reduce heat to medium-low, and stir and simmer another 2–3 minutes, until slightly thickened. The sauce will remain somewhat thin.

Meanwhile, cook the ravioli in rapidly boiling water 4–8 minutes. Ravioli made from homemade pasta dough will be done when they float to the top and pasta is al dente. If you have used wonton wrappers, the ravioli will be done when the wrappers turn from translucent to opaque and are tender. Gently remove the ravioli from the water with a skimmer or slotted spoon and drain well.

Distribute the ravioli among 4 warmed, shallow individual-serving bowls and top evenly with the sauce, using a rubber spatula to remove all the sauce from the pan. Dust with the Parmesan cheese. Garnish each serving with whole basil leaves, if you like.

Each serving provides:

360	Calories	44 g	Carbohydrate
11 g	Protein	397 mg	Sodium
15 g	Fat	99 mg	Cholesterol
3 g	Dietary Fiber		

Potato, Chard, and Gruyère Ravioli with Sage Butter

Gruyère type cheese is not uncommon in the regions of Italy that border on Switzerland. The Italians call it groviera. *We use Gruyère in this special-occasion dish since it is readily available and its flavor combines well with those of potatoes, chard, and sage. The potatoes for the filling are steamed rather than boiled so they will be less watery. You may use homemade pasta or, if time is short, purchase a 1-pound package of fresh wonton wrappers at the supermarket.*

Yield: 6 main-course servings

The filling

Russet potatoes	2	medium (1 pound)
Fresh chard	¾	pound
Gruyère cheese, shredded	2	ounces (½ cup)
Lowfat milk	¼	cup
Fresh-squeezed lemon juice	2	teaspoons
Garlic	2	cloves, minced
Freshly grated nutmeg	¼	teaspoon
Salt	⅛	teaspoon
Pepper		A few grinds

The pasta

Fresh Homemade Pasta (or 1 pound fresh wonton wrappers)	1	recipe

The sauce

Unsalted butter	3	**tablespoons**
Fresh sage leaves, slivered	3	**tablespoons**
Parmesan cheese, freshly		
grated	⅓	**cup**

Place the unpeeled potatoes on a steamer tray over 2 inches of cold water. Turn the burner on to medium-high and cook for 30 minutes, until the potatoes are very tender. Remove them from the pan and set aside for a few minutes to cool.

Meanwhile, remove the chard stems from the leaves and reserve them for another use, such as soup stock. Wash the chard leaves, but do not dry them. Place the wet leaves in a saucepan or skillet, cover, and cook over medium heat 5–7 minutes, until they have completely wilted. Drain and wrap the cooked chard in a clean tea towel. When cool enough to handle, squeeze the chard firmly in the towel to remove as much liquid as possible. Finely mince the chard.

When the potatoes are cool enough to handle, peel them and combine them in a large bowl with the chard, Gruyère, milk, lemon juice, garlic, nutmeg, salt, and pepper. Stir until well combined. The filling should have the consistency of thick mashed potatoes. If it seems too dry and crumbly, add another tablespoon or two of milk. Set the filling aside at room temperature.

If you want to use homemade pasta, prepare the Fresh Homemade Pasta and fill the ravioli according to the directions on page 171.

Otherwise, use a 1-pound package of fresh wonton wrappers from the supermarket. Lay several wrappers side by side on a lightly floured work surface. Place a heaping teaspoon of filling at the center of each, moisten the edges with water, and top each one with another wrapper. Press all around the filling with your fingers, expelling any trapped air, then press around the edge of each ravioli with a fork to completely seal in the filling. Set the filled ravioli aside on a lightly floured surface; don't allow them to touch or they will stick together. Cover with a dry towel while you fill the remaining ravioli. Proceed until you have used all the filling. (You may keep them on the counter for an hour or so at this point. Instructions for refrigerating or freezing ravioli are given in the Tips and Tools section at the beginning of the chapter on page 140.)

Meanwhile, bring several quarts of water to a rapid boil. Carefully drop the ravioli into the boiling water and cook 4–8 minutes. Ravioli made from homemade pasta dough will be done when they float to the top and are tender. If you have used wonton wrappers, the ravioli will be done when the wrappers turn from translucent to opaque and are tender.

While the ravioli are cooking, melt the butter over medium-low heat in a large skillet. When it is almost entirely melted, add the sage and stir for 2–3 minutes, until the butter barely begins to brown. Watch carefully and keep the contents of the pan moving so the butter doesn't burn. Turn off the heat.

When the ravioli are cooked, remove them gently with a skimmer or slotted spoon and drain them thoroughly. Add them to the butter in the skillet, along with the Parmesan. Stir gently to coat, then transfer to a warmed serving platter. Use a rubber spatula to get all the butter, sage, and cheese bits out of the pan. You may garnish the plate with sage leaves or minced parsley, if you wish. Serve very hot.

Each serving provides:

336	Calories	42 g	Carbohydrate
12 g	Protein	205 mg	Sodium
13 g	Fat	102 mg	Cholesterol
2 g	Dietary Fiber		

Spinach and Goat Cheese Ravioli with Creamy Walnut Sauce

We love ravioli and prepare them often. They are especially good when produced with homemade pasta, but you may take a shortcut by using commercially prepared fresh wonton wrappers instead. We have never found Italian-style goat cheese (caprino) in our markets, so this filling is made with a French feta cheese, which has a milder, less salty flavor than the Greek variety.

Yield: 6 main-course servings

The sauce
Creamy Walnut Sauce	1	cup

The pasta
Fresh Homemade Pasta (or 1 pound fresh wonton wrappers)	1	recipe

The filling
Frozen spinach, thawed	10	ounces
French feta cheese, crumbled	4	ounces (1 cup)
Egg	1	large, beaten
Garlic	2	cloves, minced
Salt	¼	teaspoon
Pepper		A few grinds

The topping

Fresh tomatoes	1	pound
		(2 medium)
Fresh-squeezed lemon juice	1	tablespoon
Salt	⅛	teaspoon
Pepper		A few grinds

Prepare the Creamy Walnut Sauce according to the directions on page 126. The surplus sauce can be kept in a closed container in the refrigerator for a few days.

Prepare the Fresh Homemade Pasta according to the directions on page 169, up to the resting stage. (Alternatively, you may use fresh wonton wrappers from the supermarket.)

While the dough is resting, squeeze the spinach with your hands to remove as much water as possible. Chop it coarsely and place in a bowl. Mix in the cheese, egg, garlic, ¼ teaspoon of salt, and pepper.

Bring several quarts of water to a rapid boil while you roll out the pasta dough and fill the ravioli according to the directions on page 171.

If you are using wonton wrappers, lay several wrappers side by side on a lightly floured work surface. Place a heaping teaspoon of filling at the center of each, moisten the edges with water, and top each one with another wrapper. Press all around the filling with your fingers, expelling any trapped air, then press around the edge of each ravioli with a fork to completely seal in the filling. Set the filled ravioli aside on a lightly floured surface; don't allow them to touch or they will stick together. Cover with a dry towel while you fill the remaining ravioli. (You may keep them on the counter for an hour or so at this point. Instructions for refrigerating or freezing ravioli are given in the Tips and Tools section at the beginning of the chapter on page 140.)

Dice the tomatoes and combine them with the lemon juice, ⅛ teaspoon of salt, and pepper. Set aside. Cook the ravioli 4–8 minutes. Ravioli made with homemade dough will be done when they float to the top and pasta is al dente. If you have used wonton wrappers, the ravioli will be done when the wrappers turn from translucent to opaque and are al dente.

Place the walnut sauce in a small pan and heat through. Keep it warm on the stove or in a double boiler. Carefully remove the cooked ravioli with a skimmer or slotted spoon, drain thoroughly, and place in warmed, shallow individual-serving bowls. Pour the sauce on top and sprinkle with the chopped tomatoes. Serve immediately.

Each serving provides:

429	Calories	43 g	Carbohydrate
16 g	Protein	473 mg	Sodium
23 g	Fat	126 mg	Cholesterol
4 g	Dietary Fiber		

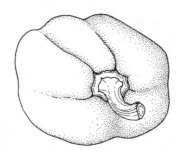

Broccoli Walnut Cannelloni with Tomato Besciamella

Cannelloni is rarely on our tables because it is time-consuming to prepare, but what a treat it is! To reduce the preparation time, you may make up the sauce the day before and buy a 1-pound package of egg roll wrappers to use in place of the homemade pasta.

Yield: 6 main-course servings

The sauce

Whole tomatoes	1	28-ounce can
Olive oil	1	tablespoon
Fresh Italian parsley, minced	⅓	cup
Garlic	2	cloves, minced
Salt	¼	teaspoon
Pepper		Several grinds
Light besciamella (see page 133)	1	cup

The filling

Raw, unsalted walnuts	¾	cup
Fresh broccoli	1	pound
Olive oil	1	tablespoon
White onion, chopped	1	large
Garlic	1	clove, minced
Salt	½	teaspoon
Italian Vegetable Stock or dry white wine	1	cup
Coarse dry bread crumbs	1	cup
Part-skim ricotta cheese	1	cup
Fresh oregano leaves, minced	1	tablespoon
Pepper		Several grinds

The pasta
 Fresh Homemade Pasta
 (or 1 pound fresh wonton
 wrappers)   1   recipe

For the casserole
 Butter   1   teaspoon
 Romano cheese, finely grated   ¼   cup

Make the sauce first. Drain the canned tomatoes, reserving the juice for another use, such as soup. Puree the tomatoes in a blender or food processor. Heat the olive oil in a sauté pan over medium heat. Add the garlic and parsley; stir and sauté for 1 minute. Add the tomato puree, salt, and pepper. Reduce heat to medium-low and cook for 15 minutes, stirring frequently. Stir in the light besciamella, cover, and set the sauce aside. (Sauce may be made a day ahead of time; refrigerate in a closed container and bring to room temperature before using.)

Make the filling next. Toast the walnuts (see page 31), finely chop them, and set aside. Separate the broccoli florets from the stalks. Finely chop the florets. Peel the stalks down to the white center, and finely dice. Set the chopped broccoli aside.

Heat 1 tablespoon of oil in a pan over medium heat and sauté the onion for 5 minutes, stirring occasionally. Add the chopped broccoli, garlic, and ¼ teaspoon of salt, and sauté, stirring often, 5 minutes. Add the stock and immediately cover the pan. Cook 5 minutes, until broccoli is tender and most of the liquid has evaporated.

In a large bowl, combine the broccoli mixture with the walnuts, bread crumbs, ricotta cheese, oregano, ¼ teaspoon of salt, and pepper. If the mixture appears too dry and crumbly, add more stock 1 tablespoon at a time to achieve a sticky consistency. (Filling may be made a day in advance; refrigerate in a closed container and bring to room temperature before using.)

About 2 hours before serving time, make the Fresh Home-made Pasta according to the directions on page 169, cutting the sheets of pasta into rectangles about 5 inches wide and 8 inches long. Meanwhile, bring several quarts of water to a boil in a large stockpot. Fill a large bowl with cold water and place it in a handy spot near the boiling pot. Spread a few clean, dry towels on the work surface. Drop the pasta sheets into the boiling water 2 at a time, cooking only 30 seconds. Remove the pasta sheets with a skimmer or slotted spoon, plunge them briefly into the cold water, drain well, and set on the towels in a single layer to dry. Precook all the pasta sheets in this manner.

Preheat the oven to 400 degrees F. Use the butter to generously coat a 9 × 13-inch baking pan or casserole dish. Cover the bottom of the dish evenly with ¼ cup of the sauce.

Place 2 tablespoons of sauce on a clean dinner plate. Place a pasta sheet on the plate and rotate the pasta to coat the underside lightly with sauce. Now place about ⅓ cup of filling on the pasta sheet and spread it out to cover the pasta thinly, leaving a ½-inch border all around. Fold the border of plain pasta over the filling at one of the narrow ends and roll the sheet up jelly-roll fashion. Carefully place the roll in the baking dish seam side down. Continue until all the pasta sheets have been filled, rolled, and placed in the dish. It is fine if the cannelloni fit tightly into the pan, but do not overlap them. You should have 12 cannelloni in the dish.

Pour the sauce evenly over the casserole and shake the dish to settle it a bit. Top evenly with the Romano cheese and bake 20 minutes. Allow to cool 10 minutes before serving.

Each serving provides:

346	Calories	25 g	Carbohydrate
14 g	Protein	744 mg	Sodium
23 g	Fat	31 mg	Cholesterol
5 g	Dietary Fiber		

Riso, Polenta, and Gnocchi

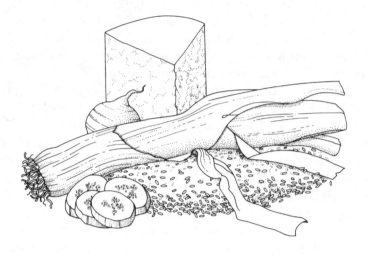

In Northern Italy, the first course of the day's main meal is likely to be rice, polenta, or gnocchi. These dishes play as important a role in the diet of the north as pasta does in the south. The time-tested preparation techniques for these classic foods are quite simple once you learn the basics.

Northern Italians grow wonderful specialty rices and have an inspired repertoire of rice preparations, the most famous of which is risotto. Risotto uses a unique oval, short-grained rice—usually *fino Arborio*—that releases its starch gradually during the cooking process to create a creamy texture. This comfort-food quality makes risotto a frequent choice for us, and we think you'll agree that these dishes are delicious enough to be prepared often.

In addition to several wonderful risotto preparations, we have included in this chapter an Italian-style rice pilaf and a traditional Roman rice croquette.

Polenta—basically cornmeal mush elevated to gastronomic heights by innovative seasonings and toppings—is served either creamy and soft or firm. Soft polenta, made from fine yellow cornmeal, is always served hot and usually seasoned with cheese and butter. The firm style is made from coarse yellow cornmeal, shaped in a loaf or patty, sliced, and then baked, fried, or grilled. It can be served hot or at room temperature, with or without a sauce. Polenta is a tasty, hearty, and nutritious food, and we eat it with pleasure on a regular basis.

Gnocchi are bite-size dumplings that melt in your mouth. Nothing compares to them. They are typically made with semolina, potatoes, or ricotta cheese. Once you learn the simple but little-known process of gnocchi-making, you will prepare these delectable morsels often.

Contrary to Italian tradition, we often center a meal around rice, polenta, or gnocchi. Alongside pasta, these dishes belong at the heart of meatless Italian cuisine. They are versatile, satisfying, economical, and absolutely scrumptious. *Buon appetito!*

Tips and Tools for Risotto

- Don't rinse Arborio rice before cooking as you don't want to wash away any of the surface starches.
- To prevent sticking or scorching, stir risotto almost constantly as it absorbs each addition of liquid. If risotto sticks despite stirring, reduce the heat slightly. Since risotto requires vigilant stirring, you may want to enlist the help of a friend or family member.

- The speed with which risotto cooks is affected by type of cookware, variations in individual stove temperature, and altitude. You may need to adjust the cooking time and the amount of liquid accordingly.
- If the liquid is absorbed before the rice is tender, add more hot stock or water, ½ cup at a time, until the rice is tender and the consistency of the risotto is creamy, not sticky.

Tips and Tools for Polenta

- Some polenta cooks prefer fine cornmeal for soft polenta dishes and the coarse variety for firm polenta dishes. Some even mix the two to achieve a medium textured polenta. If you are purchasing cornmeal for polenta at an Italian specialty store, it is likely to be labeled simply "polenta." Obviously, personal preference plays a role in this decision, so use whatever type of cornmeal you like.
- Traditional Italian cooks make polenta in a heavy copper kettle—called a *paiolo*—that is reserved exclusively for this purpose. In our kitchens, a heavy-bottomed stainless-steel or enameled cast-iron saucepan works well.
- Essential tools include a whisk for adding the cornmeal to the water and a long-handled wooden spoon for stirring as the polenta thickens.
- To avoid lumps in polenta, add the cornmeal to the hot water gradually, over the course of a minute or two, pouring in a slow, steady stream. Whisk continuously while you are adding the cornmeal to the water.
- Polenta will stiffen as it cools. For dishes where a firm texture is desired, pour the cooked polenta into a shallow pan or mound it on a board, smooth the surface with a wet spatula, and allow to cool. The polenta can then be sliced for grilling or layering in a casserole.

- For firm polenta dishes, the polenta can be made up to a few days ahead of time. Pour the hot polenta into a loaf pan or other baking dish, cover tightly with plastic wrap, and refrigerate until needed.

- It is easier than it first appears to clean the pot used for cooking polenta. Fill it with cold water and set it aside for a few hours. The sticky polenta will soften as it absorbs the water and can then be removed easily.

Tips and Tools for Gnocchi

- Gnocchi can be prepared ahead of time. Dust them with flour, cover with a tea towel, and hold at room temperature for 1–2 hours before cooking. To refrigerate or freeze them for longer periods, distribute on a baking sheet far enough apart so they don't touch. Once frozen, they can be transferred to a plastic bag.

- Since it takes less than 5 minutes to cook gnocchi, don't cook them in advance. They will become tough and rubbery as they dry.

- Be careful not to overcook gnocchi. If they absorb too much water during cooking, they will be tough and heavy.

- Make sure your sauce is ready when the cooked gnocchi come out of the pot. You can always let the sauce sit for a while—it can even be reheated if necessary. Cooked gnocchi, on the other hand, must be tossed with the sauce and served immediately.

- Use a skimmer, flat metal strainer, or large slotted spoon to remove cooked gnocchi from the pot, draining them well as you do so.

Risotto with Fresh Fennel and Carrots

VEGAN

The essence of Italian country cooking is expressed in this simple risotto dish. The vegetables of midwinter are wrapped up in warm, creamy rice. Fennel is a member of the parsley family that looks similar to celery and has a pronounced licorice flavor. It appears often in Italian recipes.

Yield: 4 main-course servings

Italian Vegetable Stock*	3½	**cups**
Brandy	2	**tablespoons**
Fresh fennel bulb, diced	1½	**cups**
Carrot	1	**medium, diced**
Yellow onion, chopped	½	**cup**
Olive oil	2	**tablespoons**
Arborio rice, uncooked	1	**cup**
Dried basil	1	**teaspoon**
Fresh Italian parsley, minced	¼	**cup**

Heat the stock in a saucepan until just steaming and keep handy near the stove. Place the brandy and 2 tablespoons of the stock in a 2-quart pot that has a tight fitting lid over medium heat. Add the fennel, carrot, and onion. Stir to coat, cover, and cook for 10 minutes, removing the lid occasionally to stir the vegetables around.

Meanwhile, heat the oil in a heavy-bottomed saucepan over medium heat and add the rice. Stir to coat the rice with the oil,

*If you do not have Italian Vegetable Stock on hand, make some according to the directions on page 34, or dissolve 1 large, low-sodium vegetable broth cube in 3½ cups of hot water.

then add about ½ cup of the stock and the basil, and stir constantly until the liquid is almost completely absorbed. Add the remaining stock ½ cup at a time, stirring almost constantly and waiting until the liquid is almost completely absorbed before each addition. Add the braised vegetables and parsley with the last ½ cup of stock. When the last addition of stock has been absorbed and the rice is tender, transfer to a warmed serving bowl. Garnish with parsley or fennel sprigs.

Each serving provides:

297	Calories	51 g	Carbohydrate
4 g	Protein	188 mg	Sodium
7 g	Fat	0 mg	Cholesterol
2 g	Dietary Fiber		

Risotto with Winter Vegetables and Fresh Sage

VEGAN

This risotto has an earthy quality. The root vegetables combine wonderfully with the sage. Serve this as a main dish with a salad, bread, and Gorgonzola cheese, or as a first course or side dish for 6 as part of a multicourse meal.

Yield: 4 main-course servings

Italian Vegetable Stock*	3½	**cups**
Leek	1	**large**
		(½ pound)
Olive oil	2	**tablespoons**
Garlic	2	**cloves, minced**
Carrot	1	**medium, diced**
Turnip	1	**medium, diced**
Red wine	½	**cup**
Arborio rice, uncooked	1	**cup**
Whole pear tomatoes	1	**16-ounce can**
Fresh sage, minced	2	**tablespoons**
Salt	¼	**teaspoon**
Pepper		**Several grinds**

Heat the stock in a saucepan until just steaming and keep handy near the stove. Cut off and discard the tough green tops from the leek. Slice the leek in half lengthwise and carefully wash away any sand or dirt caught in the layers. Dice and set aside.

*If you do not have Italian Vegetable Stock on hand, make some according to the directions on page 34, or dissolve 1 large, low-sodium vegetable broth cube in 3½ cups of hot water.

Drain the juice from the can of tomatoes into a bowl. Chop the tomatoes into another bowl to catch their juices. Set aside. Heat the oil in a large skillet over medium heat. Sauté the garlic and leek for about 5 minutes, then add the tomato juice and ½ cup of water. Stir in the diced carrot and turnip, cover, and cook for about 25 minutes until the vegetables are fork-tender. Stir occasionally during the cooking time to ensure that they do not stick to the bottom of the pan.

Meanwhile, place the wine in a large, heavy-bottomed saucepan. Heat over medium heat and stir in the rice. Cook, stirring constantly until the wine is almost completely absorbed. Add ½ cup of the stock at a time, stirring almost constantly and waiting until the liquid is almost completely absorbed before each addition. Add the sage, salt, pepper, chopped tomatoes, and cooked vegetables with the last ½ cup of stock. When the liquid is absorbed and the rice is tender, serve immediately.

Each serving provides:

329	Calories	58 g	Carbohydrate
5 g	Protein	525 mg	Sodium
8 g	Fat	0 mg	Cholesterol
3 g	Dietary Fiber		

Risotto with Roasted Peppers and Blood Oranges

VEGAN

Blood oranges appear in markets all over Italy every spring. Their skin has a slight red blush. The fruit inside is quite red and its flavor is a cross between an orange and a grapefruit. These oranges are cultivated in the United States and appear in Italian groceries and many large supermarkets. In this recipe, their subtle sweetness enhances the smoky flavor of the peppers and the basil. You will need 3–4 blood oranges for this recipe.

Yield: 4 main-course servings

Italian Vegetable Stock*	3½ cups
Red bell pepper	1 medium
Yellow bell pepper	1 medium
Olive oil	1 tablespoon
Green onions	3, thinly sliced
Arborio rice, uncooked	1 cup
Juice of blood oranges	½ cup
Blood orange	1 medium
Fresh Italian parsley, minced	¼ cup
Fresh basil leaves, minced	¼ cup

Heat the stock in a saucepan until just steaming and keep handy near the stove. Prepare a gas or electric grill to medium-high or preheat the broiler. Remove the stem ends from the peppers and cut them into quarters. Remove the seeds and membranes.

*If you do not have Italian Vegetable Stock on hand, make some according to the directions on page 34, or dissolve 1 large, low-sodium vegetable broth cube in 3½ cups of hot water.

Place the peppers on the grill or under the broiler and cook for 5 minutes, until slightly charred. Turn and cook an additional 5 minutes. Remove to a plate and, when cool enough to handle, cut them into thin strips and set aside in a warm place. Peel 1 orange and divide it into wedges. Peel the wedges and break the orange segments in half. Set aside.

Heat the oil over medium in a heavy-bottomed saucepan. Add the green onions and sauté for about 1 minute, then add the rice and stir to coat for about 1 minute. Add the orange juice and cook, stirring constantly, until it is almost completely absorbed. Add the stock, ½ cup at a time, stirring almost constantly and waiting until nearly all the liquid is absorbed before each addition. Add the orange segments, parsley, and basil with the last ½ cup of stock. When this last addition of stock has been absorbed and the rice is tender, transfer to a preheated serving dish and top with the pepper strips. Serve immediately.

Each serving provides:

281	Calories	56 g	Carbohydrate
5 g	Protein	166 mg	Sodium
4 g	Fat	0 mg	Cholesterol
3 g	Dietary Fiber		

Sautéed Portobello Mushrooms with Risotto

Meaty portobello mushrooms, which can be found in many well-stocked grocery stores or Italian markets, develop a delightful flavor when sautéed with butter and balsamic vinegar. The enjoyment of this dish begins with its visual appeal: the risotto is topped with the mushrooms, scarlet radicchio, and bright green parsley.

Yield: 6 first-course or side-dish servings

Portobello mushrooms	¾	pound
Unsalted butter	2	tablespoons
Garlic	3	cloves, minced
Balsamic vinegar	2	tablespoons
Fresh-squeezed lemon juice	2	tablespoons
Dried thyme	1	teaspoon
Italian Vegetable Stock*	3½	cups
Olive oil	1	tablespoon
Dry sherry	1	tablespoon
Arborio rice, uncooked	1	cup
Fresh Italian parsley, minced	½	cup
Radicchio, chopped	1	cup

Gently clean the mushrooms with a brush or soft cloth. Trim off and discard the bottoms of the stems and remove the stems from the caps. Slice the mushroom caps into ¼-inch strips. Cut the stems in half lengthwise, then into quarters or eighths, depending on their size. Melt the butter in a large skillet and

---

*If you do not have Italian Vegetable Stock on hand, make some according to the directions on page 34, or dissolve 1 large, low-sodium vegetable broth cube in 3½ cups of hot water.

add the garlic. Sauté for 1 minute, then add the mushrooms, balsamic vinegar, lemon juice, and thyme. Sauté, stirring frequently, for about 20 minutes, until the mushrooms are tender and their liquid has reduced.

Meanwhile, heat the stock in a saucepan until just steaming and keep handy near the stove. Place the oil and sherry in a heavy-bottomed saucepan over medium heat and add the rice. Stir for about 1 minute to coat the rice, then add the stock ½ cup at a time, stirring almost constantly and waiting until the liquid is almost completely absorbed before each addition. Add the parsley, reserving 1 tablespoon, with the last ½ cup of stock. When the last addition of stock has been absorbed and the rice is tender, transfer to a warmed serving bowl. Garnish with the sautéed mushroom strips, chopped radicchio, and remaining parsley. Serve immediately.

Each serving provides:

237	Calories	41 g	Carbohydrate
3 g	Protein	114 mg	Sodium
7 g	Fat	11 mg	Cholesterol
1 g	Dietary Fiber		

Risotto with Leeks,
Red Wine, and Thyme

As with most risottos, this dish can be served as a main course as indicated, or as a side dish or first course for 6. The red wine turns the rice a light pink color that highlights the leeks.

Yield: 4 main-course servings

Italian Vegetable Stock°	3½	**cups**
Leeks	3	**medium (1½ pounds)**
Unsalted butter	1	**tablespoon**
Dried thyme	1	**teaspoon**
Salt	¼	**teaspoon**
Pepper		**Several grinds**
Dry red wine	½	**cup**
Arborio rice, uncooked	1	**cup**
Fresh Italian parsley, minced	¼	**cup**

Heat the stock in a saucepan until just steaming and keep handy near the stove. Cut off and discard the tough green tops from the leeks. Slice each leek in half lengthwise and carefully wash away any sand or dirt caught in the layers. Thinly slice the halves. Melt the butter in a large cast-iron skillet over medium heat and add the leeks. Crush the thyme between the palms of your hands and add to the leeks along with the salt and pepper. Sauté for about 10 minutes, stirring occasionally. When tender but not browned, remove from the heat and set aside.

°If you do not have Italian Vegetable Stock on hand, make some according to the directions on page 34, or dissolve 1 large, low-sodium vegetable broth cube in 3½ cups of hot water.

Meanwhile, heat the wine in a heavy-bottomed saucepan over medium heat and add the rice. Stir constantly as the rice absorbs the wine, then add the stock ½ cup at a time, stirring almost constantly and waiting until the liquid is almost completely absorbed before each addition. Add the leeks and parsley with the last ½ cup of stock. When the stock has been absorbed and the rice is tender, transfer to a warmed serving bowl. Serve immediately.

Each serving provides:

287	Calories	56 g	Carbohydrate
5 g	Protein	312 mg	Sodium
4 g	Fat	8 mg	Cholesterol
2 g	Dietary Fiber		

Risotto with Baked Garlic and Fresh Oregano

The fresh oregano and sweet baked garlic combine to create an earthy, addictive risotto.

Yield: 6 first-course or main-course servings

Italian Vegetable Stock*	3½	cups
Baked garlic	1	bulb
Olive oil	1	tablespoon
Red onion	1	medium
Arborio rice, uncooked	1	cup
Red wine	½	cup
Cooked red beans**	1	cup
Fresh oregano leaves, minced	2	tablespoons
Parmesan cheese, finely grated	½	cup

Heat the stock in a saucepan until just steaming and keep handy near the stove. Bake a garlic bulb according to the directions on page 30. Squeeze the garlic paste out of the baked bulb and whisk it into the stock.

*If you do not have Italian Vegetable Stock on hand, make some according to the directions on page 34, or dissolve 1 large, low-sodium vegetable broth cube in 3½ cups of hot water.
**Cook ½ cup of presoaked dried beans for 30–45 minutes (see page 30) until they are al dente. Alternatively, you may use canned beans, rinsed and well drained.

Heat the oil in a heavy-bottomed saucepan over medium heat and sauté the onion for 2 minutes, then add the rice and stir for 1 minute to coat with oil. Add the wine and stir constantly until it is almost completely absorbed. Add the garlic-laced stock ½ cup at a time, stirring almost constantly and waiting until the liquid is almost completely absorbed before each addition. Add the beans and oregano with the last ½ cup of stock. When this last addition has been absorbed and the rice is tender, stir in the Parmesan. Serve immediately.

Each serving provides:

254	Calories	42 g	Carbohydrate
8 g	Protein	233 mg	Sodium
5 g	Fat	5 mg	Cholesterol
2 g	Dietary Fiber		

Risotto with Zucchini, Butter, Sage, and Gorgonzola

This rich, wonderful risotto combines the earthy flavor of sage with one of Italy's favorite vegetables, the zucchini. A top-quality Italian Gorgonzola will yield the best results. For a marvelous meal, serve Summer Bread Salad (page 70) as a first course, followed by this risotto and Marsala Glazed Carrots (page 244). A chilled Pinot Grigio would be an ideal accompanying beverage.

Yield: 6 main-course servings

Zucchini	¾	pound (about 3 medium)
Tomatoes	2	medium (1 pound)
Unsalted butter	2	tablespoons
Garlic	2	cloves, minced
Fresh sage leaves, slivered	¼	cup
Salt	¼	teaspoon
Pepper		Several grinds
Dry sherry	½	cup
Italian Vegetable Stock*	5½	cups
Arborio rice, uncooked	1½	cups
Gorgonzola cheese, crumbled	2	ounces (½ cup)

Trim and discard the ends of the zucchini, then cut zucchini lengthwise into ¼-inch slices. Cut the slices into ¼-inch matchsticks. Set aside. Cut the tomatoes in half crosswise and squeeze

---

*If you do not have Italian Vegetable Stock on hand, make some according to the directions on page 34, or dissolve 1½ large, low-sodium vegetable cubes in 5½ cups of hot water.

out and discard their juicy seed pockets. Dice the tomatoes and set aside.

Melt 1 tablespoon of butter in a medium skillet over medium-high heat. Stir in the sage and 1 clove of the garlic, then add the zucchini strips and salt. Stir and sauté about 5 minutes, until the zucchini gets limp and begins to brown. Stir in the tomatoes and pepper, and cook an additional 2 minutes over medium-low heat. Put a lid on the pan, remove from the heat, and set aside.

Meanwhile, heat the stock in a saucepan until just steaming and keep handy near the stove. Melt the remaining butter in a large, heavy-bottomed saucepan over medium heat and briefly sauté the remaining garlic. Add the rice and stir for about 1 minute, then add the sherry and stir constantly until it is almost completely absorbed. Add the stock ½ cup at a time, stirring almost constantly and waiting until liquid is absorbed before each addition. When the last addition of stock has been absorbed and rice is tender, stir in the cheese until it is melted and well distributed. Stir in the zucchini mixture and transfer to a warmed serving bowl or tureen for the table. Pass the pepper grinder.

Each serving provides:

309	Calories	50 g	Carbohydrate
7 g	Protein	436 mg	Sodium
8 g	Fat	19 mg	Cholesterol
2 g	Dietary Fiber		

Rice with Asparagus and Egg Lemon Sauce

This delicate, tart, and creamy dish is true comfort food. Make a meal of it when the first spring asparagus hits the market.

Yield: 4 main-course servings

Salt	½	**teaspoon**
Arborio rice, uncooked	1¾	**cups**
Fresh asparagus spears	1¼	**pounds**
Lemon zest, minced	1	**teaspoon**
Unsalted butter	1	**tablespoon**
Garlic	4	**cloves, minced**
Pepper		**Several grinds**
Dry white wine	¼	**cup**
Fresh Italian parsley, minced	¼	**cup**
Egg°	1	**large**
Fresh-squeezed lemon juice	3	**tablespoons**
Freshly grated nutmeg	1	**teaspoon**
Parmesan cheese, finely grated	¼	**cup**

Combine ¼ teaspoon of the salt with 5 cups of water in a large stockpot and bring to a boil over high heat. Add the rice and stir. When the water returns to a boil, reduce heat to medium-low and simmer, uncovered, about 25–30 minutes, until almost all the liquid has been absorbed and the rice is tender. Stir the rice frequently and vigorously as it simmers, especially toward

°Some authorities suggest avoiding dishes made with raw eggs, due to the remote possibility of salmonella contamination. Immune-compromised individuals may wish to heed this advice. For more information, contact your local office of the U.S. Department of Agriculture.

the end of the cooking time, to prevent it from sticking. The texture of the finished rice should be creamy, not sticky, so do not cook it too long. If all the liquid is absorbed before the rice is tender, add more hot water ½ cup at a time until the rice is done.

Meanwhile, break off and discard the tough stem portion of the asparagus and cut the spears at a slant into 1-inch pieces. Use a vegetable peeler to remove several very thin strips of peel from a lemon, being careful not to include any of the white portion under the peel, which has a bitter taste. Use a sharp knife to sliver the peel, then mince finely to yield 1 teaspoon of zest.

Heat the butter in a large sauté pan over medium heat. Add the garlic and stir for a moment or two, then add the asparagus, remaining ¼ teaspoon salt, and pepper. Stir and sauté 5–7 minutes, depending on the thickness of the asparagus spears. Stir in the lemon zest and parsley, then add the wine. Immediately cover the pan and remove it from the heat.

In a small bowl, beat the egg with the lemon juice, nutmeg, and Parmesan until well combined. When the rice is done, mix it in a warmed serving bowl with the egg-lemon sauce. The rice must be very hot to cook the egg somewhat. Stir in the asparagus mixture and serve immediately, passing additional cheese, if you wish.

Each serving provides:

426	Calories	77 g	Carbohydrate
12 g	Protein	416 mg	Sodium
7 g	Fat	65 mg	Cholesterol
2 g	Dietary Fiber		

Risotto alla Milanese

A specialty of Milan since early times, this simple risotto is delicately flavored with precious saffron. The result is a light, unique taste and brilliant yellow color. In Milan, this risotto typically accompanies a braised lamb shank. We enjoy it with grilled vegetables—such as eggplants and zucchini—a leafy salad, and a glass of chardonnay. For a very special dinner, include a first course such as Spiced Broth with Spinach, Mushrooms, Eggs, and Cheese (page 88).

Yield: 6 first-course or side-dish servings

Italian Vegetable Stock*	6	**cups**
Unsalted butter	2	**tablespoons**
White onion	1	**medium, diced**
Arborio rice, uncooked	1½	**cups**
Dry white wine	½	**cup**
Saffron threads	½	**teaspoon, crushed**
Salt	¼	**teaspoon**
Parmesan cheese, finely grated	¾	**cup**
Fresh Italian parsley, minced	2	**tablespoons**

Heat the stock in a saucepan until just steaming and keep it handy near the stove. Melt the butter in a large saucepan over medium heat and sauté the onion 5 minutes, until golden and translucent. Add the rice and stir for about 1 minute. Then add the wine and cook, stirring, until it is almost completely absorbed. Add the hot stock ½ cup at a time, stirring almost

---

*If you do not have Italian Vegetable Stock on hand, make some according to the directions on page 34, or dissolve 1½ large, low-sodium vegetable broth cubes in 6 cups of hot water.

constantly and waiting until the liquid is almost completely absorbed before each addition. Add the saffron and salt with the second-to-last addition of stock. When almost all the liquid has been absorbed and the rice is tender, stir in the cheese and parsley. Serve hot on warmed serving dishes.

Each serving provides:

307	Calories	49 g	Carbohydrate
8 g	Protein	460 mg	Sodium
7 g	Fat	19 mg	Cholesterol
1 g	Dietary Fiber		

Risotto with Porcini, Fresh Basil, and Pine Nuts

This risotto takes on the extraordinarily rich taste of the porcini mushrooms, which is complemented well by the bright flavors of red bell pepper and fresh basil. It is a light but very satisfying dish, which could easily carry a meal if accompanied by a first course of Fresh Mozzarella with Tomatoes and Basil (page 68), good crusty bread with Seasoned Olive Oil (page 46), steamed vegetables, and a light, tart green salad to finish.

Yield: 6 main-course servings

Italian Vegetable Stock*	7	cups
Dried porcini mushrooms	½	ounce
Pine nuts	¼	cup
Salt	¼	teaspoon
Pepper		Several grinds
Olive oil	1	tablespoon
Unsalted butter	1	tablespoon
Garlic	3	cloves, minced
Red bell pepper, finely chopped	½	cup
Arborio rice, uncooked	2	cups
Dry white wine	½	cup
Fresh basil leaves, chopped	⅓	cup
Parmesan cheese, finely grated	⅓	cup
Fresh-squeezed lemon juice	1	tablespoon

*If you do not have Italian Vegetable Stock on hand, make some according to the directions on page 34, or dissolve 2 large, low-sodium vegetable broth cubes in 7 cups of hot water.

Riso, Polenta, and Gnocchi

Heat the stock in a saucepan until just steaming. Soak the dried porcini in the hot stock for 30 minutes, then lift them out, reserving the stock. Chop the mushrooms and set aside. Strain the stock through a paper coffee filter. Return it to the saucepan, add the salt and pepper, heat to steaming, and and keep it handy near the stove.

Heat the olive oil and butter in a heavy-bottomed saucepan over medium heat. Sauté the garlic and bell pepper for about 5 minutes, then add the rice and stir for 1 minute to coat with oil and seasonings. Add the wine and stir constantly until it is almost completely absorbed. Add the stock ½ cup at a time, stirring almost constantly and waiting until liquid is absorbed before each addition. Add the basil with the last ½ cup of broth. When the last addition of broth has been absorbed and rice is tender, stir in the pine nuts, Parmesan, and lemon juice. Serve immediately.

Each serving provides:

376	Calories	62 g	Carbohydrate
8 g	Protein	387 mg	Sodium
9 g	Fat	9 mg	Cholesterol
1 g	Dietary Fiber		

Artichoke Oregano Risotto
Baked in Pepper Shells

Though this recipe has several steps, it is actually quite simple to prepare, and a delicious treat for friends and family. You may use bell peppers of any color. This recipe calls for water-packed canned artichokes, though fresh artichokes may be used. Purchase 2 pounds and prepare according to the directions on page 78.

Yield: 4 main-course servings

Pine nuts	1	**tablespoon**
Italian Vegetable Stock*	5	**cups**
Arborio rice, uncooked	1½	**cups**
Salt	¼	**teaspoon**
Olive oil	1	**tablespoon plus ½ teaspoon**
Dried red chili flakes	¼	**teaspoon**
White onion	1	**medium, diced**
Carrot	1	**medium, diced**
Fresh Italian parsley, minced	¼	**cup**
Garlic	2	**cloves, minced**
Canned artichoke hearts	1	**8½-ounce can (drained wt.)**
Dried oregano	2	**teaspoons**
Bell peppers	4	**medium**
Fresh-squeezed lemon juice	1	**tablespoon**
Parmesan cheese, finely grated	¼	**cup**
Part-skim mozzarella, shredded	1½	**ounces (⅓ cup)**

*If you do not have Italian Vegetable Stock on hand, make up a batch according to the directions on page 34, or dissolve 2 large, low-sodium vegetable broth cubes in 5 cups of hot water.

Toast the pine nuts (see page 31), chop them coarsely, and set aside.

Bring the stock with ⅛ teaspoon of the salt to a boil over high heat. Add the rice and stir. When stock returns to a boil, reduce heat to medium-low and simmer, uncovered, about 25–30 minutes, until almost all the liquid has been absorbed and the rice is tender. Stir the rice frequently and vigorously as it simmers, especially toward the end of the cooking time, to prevent it from sticking. The texture of the finished rice should be creamy, not sticky, so do not overcook. If all the liquid is absorbed before the rice is tender, add more hot stock or water ½ cup at a time until the rice is done.

Meanwhile, heat 1 tablespoon of the olive oil over medium heat and sauté the chili flakes for a moment, then add the onion, carrot, and parsley. Stir and sauté 5 minutes. Add the garlic, drained artichoke hearts, oregano, and remaining ⅛ teaspoon salt. Sauté, stirring occasionally, 10 minutes. Turn off the heat and keep the artichoke mixture in the hot pan.

Meanwhile, preheat the broiler. Cut the peppers in half lengthwise and discard the stems, seeds, and white membranes. Place the pepper halves cut side down on the broiler pan and broil 2 inches from the flame for 5–7 minutes, until well charred. Cool for several minutes, then peel off as much of the skin as possible. Replace on the broiler pan, cut side up, and broil an additional 3 minutes.

Turn off the broiler and preheat the oven to 375 degrees F. Transfer the peppers, cut side up, to a baking sheet rubbed with ½ teaspoon of olive oil. When the rice is done, combine it with the artichoke mixture, lemon juice, Parmesan, and toasted pine nuts. Stir to distribute everything evenly. Mound the mixture into the pepper halves. Top evenly with mozzarella. Bake 15–20 minutes, until the cheese is browned and bubbling. Serve hot.

Each serving provides:

466	Calories	83 g	Carbohydrate
13 g	Protein	687 mg	Sodium
9 g	Fat	10 mg	Cholesterol
4 g	Dietary Fiber		

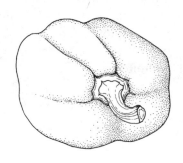

Rice Croquettes with Mozzarella Centers

In Italian, these treasures are called supplì al telefono—telephone wires—because of the strings formed by the melted mozzarella when you bite into them. Traditionally, supplì are deep-fried; however, baking achieves a crisp exterior without contributing unnecessary oil. This is a classic way to use leftover cooked risotto (it takes 3 cups), but if you come to love these croquettes as we do, you will be happy to cook rice just for this purpose. You may also use any leftover tomato sauce in place of the tomato puree. The croquettes store well in a sealed container in the refrigerator; reheat them in a toaster oven to maintain their crispness. Serve them as a fun and flavorful side dish or as the first course of any Italian-style meal. The children at your dinner table will particularly enjoy them. They are also great to take along on a picnic.

Yield: 8 first-course or side-dish servings

Italian Vegetable Stock[*]	**3½ cups**
Arborio rice, uncooked	**1 cup**
Parmesan cheese, finely grated	**⅓ cup**
Olive oil	**2 tablespoons plus ½ teaspoon**

[*]If you do not have Italian Vegetable Stock on hand, make some according to the directions on page 34, or dissolve 1 large, low-sodium vegetable broth cube in 3½ cups of hot water.

Tomato puree	¾	cup
Egg	1	medium
Dried basil	2	teaspoons
Garlic	1	clove, minced
Salt		A pinch
Pepper		Several grinds
Part-skim mozzarella	2	ounces
Fine dry bread crumbs	1	cup

Make the risotto first. Bring the stock to a boil in a saucepan and add the rice. Bring back to a boil over high heat, then reduce heat to medium-low and cook 25–30 minutes, stirring frequently and vigorously, especially toward the end of the cooking time. Rice is done when it has absorbed almost all the liquid and is tender. If liquid is gone before the rice is tender, add more stock ½ cup at a time until the rice is done. Consistency should be sticky and thick. Stir in the Parmesan and set aside to cool.

Rub ½ teaspoon of olive oil over a baking sheet; preheat the oven to 400 degrees F. When risotto is cooled, combine it in a bowl with the tomato puree, egg, basil, garlic, salt, and pepper.

Cut the mozzarella cheese into 16 cubes. Place the bread crumbs on a large plate. Pour 2 tablespoons of olive oil onto a small plate and rub a bit of it on your palms. Using your hands, form the rice into balls slightly smaller than golf balls. Poke a hole into the middle of each ball with your finger, and insert a cube of mozzarella. Close the rice mixture around the cheese to seal it in, and roll each ball in crumbs to coat lightly. Place the balls on the oiled baking sheet, about 1 inch apart. Oil your hands as needed to prevent sticking. Continue until you have formed 16 balls of equal size. Bake until well browned and sizzling, 15–20 minutes. Serve hot or at room temperature.

Each serving provides:

240	Calories	35 g	Carbohydrate
8 g	Protein	383 mg	Sodium
7 g	Fat	35 mg	Cholesterol
1 g	Dietary Fiber		

Baked Rice with Tomatoes, Olives, and Capers

VEGAN

This Italian-style pilaf comes together quickly and easily. It makes a wonderful first course or side dish, but can also serve as a main dish for lunch or a light supper. We have called for the richly flavored dry oil-cured black olives; however, you can substitute another distinctive type, such as a spiced green olive. If you do use brined olives, rinse them before mincing so the flavor of the vinegar is not overpowering. A generous portion of grilled or steamed vegetables topped with Garlic Maionese (see page 136) would be wonderful with the pilaf. Prepare this dish in a pan that is suitable for both stove-top cooking and baking, such as a cast-iron Dutch oven or a heavy-bottomed stainless-steel skillet with no plastic parts.

Yield: 6 first-course or side-dish servings

Whole pear tomatoes	1	**28-ounce can**
Italian Vegetable Stock	3	**cups**
Olive oil	1	**tablespoon**
White onion	1	**large, diced**
Dried red chili flakes	¼	**teaspoon**
Long-grain white rice	1¾	**cups**
Dry oil-cured black olives, pitted and chopped	3	**tablespoons**
Bay leaves	2	**large**
Capers, drained	2	**tablespoons**

°If you do not have Italian Vegetable Stock on hand, make up a batch according to the directions on page 34, or dissolve 1 large, low-sodium vegetable broth cube in 3 cups of hot water.

Preheat the oven to 375 degrees F. Drain the juice from the tomatoes and reserve for another use, such as soup. Chop the tomatoes coarsely into a bowl and set aside. Bring the stock to a boil in a saucepan.

Meanwhile, heat the olive oil over medium heat in an oven-proof pan. Sauté the onion and chili flakes for 3–5 minutes, stirring frequently, until the onion is opaque and golden. Add the rice and sauté, stirring frequently, for 3 minutes. Add the boiling stock, tomatoes, olives, and bay leaves. Bring to a boil over medium-high heat, then transfer the pan to the oven and bake, uncovered, 20 minutes. Mound the rice in a warmed serving bowl and toss with the capers. Serve hot or warm.

Each serving provides:

289	Calories	56 g	Carbohydrate
5 g	Protein	491 mg	Sodium
5 g	Fat	0 mg	Cholesterol
2 g	Dietary Fiber		

Soft Polenta with Gorgonzola, Oregano, and Rosemary

This soft-style polenta is a wonderful companion dish to a grilled entrée. The interplay of the oregano and rosemary with the Gorgonzola cheese has delicious results. Any leftover polenta can be formed into patties, grilled or panfried at a later time, and served as an antipasto.

Yield: 6 first-course or side-dish servings

Water	2	**cups**
Salt	¼	**teaspoon**
Dried oregano	1	**teaspoon**
Dried rosemary	½	**teaspoon**
Yellow cornmeal	½	**cup**
Unsalted butter	1	**tablespoon**
Gorgonzola cheese, crumbled	1½	**ounces (¼ cup)**

Heat the water to a simmer over medium-high heat in a heavy-bottomed saucepan. Crush the oregano and rosemary with a mortar and pestle until very fine, or thoroughly crumble with your fingers. Add the herbs and salt to the water. Gradually pour in the cornmeal in a slow, steady stream, whisking constantly. Reduce the heat to medium-low and gently simmer about 20 minutes, stirring almost constantly with a wooden spoon. As it cooks, the polenta will become thick. When it is thick enough to pull away from the sides of the pan, it is done. Stir in the butter and cheese. Serve immediately, or keep warm in a double boiler over medium heat. Stir in a tablespoon of hot water just before serving if the polenta appears too thick.

Each serving provides:

85	Calories	9 g	Carbohydrate
2 g	Protein	217 mg	Sodium
4 g	Fat	13 mg	Cholesterol
1 g	Dietary Fiber		

Polenta with Romano Cheese and Olive Mint Tomato Sauce

This dish combines the sweetness of cornmeal, tomatoes, and mint with the bitterness of dry oil-cured Italian olives. The effect is rich and satisfying—a perfect, simple supper for a chilly evening. Serve it with dry red wine and a leafy, tart salad.

Yield: 6 main-course servings

Yellow onion	1	small
Olive oil	1	tablespoon
Garlic	2	cloves, minced
Crushed tomatoes	1	28-ounce can
Dried marjoram	½	teaspoon
Salt	¼	teaspoon plus ⅛ teaspoon
Pepper		Several grinds
Dry red wine	¼	cup
Dry oil-cured black olives, pitted and minced	⅓	cup
Fresh mint leaves, minced	½	cup
Italian Vegetable Stock*	6	cups
Yellow cornmeal	1½	cups
Romano cheese, finely grated	½	cup

Peel the onion and cut it in half lengthwise, then cut each half crosswise into thin slices. Heat the olive oil in a skillet over medium heat and sauté the onion and garlic for 2 minutes. Add

*If you do not have any Italian Vegetable Stock on hand, make up a batch using the recipe on page 34, or dissolve 2 large, low-sodium vegetable broth cubes in 6 cups of hot water and omit the additional salt.

the tomatoes, marjoram, ¼ teaspoon of salt, and pepper. Bring to a simmer, reduce heat to medium-low, and cook for 5 minutes. Stir in the wine, reduce heat to low, and simmer 10 minutes. Stir in the olives and mint, cover, and set aside.

Meanwhile, combine the stock and ⅛ teaspoon of salt in a large saucepan and bring to a boil over high heat. Gradually pour in the cornmeal in a slow, steady stream, whisking constantly. Reduce the heat to medium-low and gently simmer about 20 minutes, stirring almost constantly with a wooden spoon. The polenta will thicken as it cooks. When it is thick enough to pull away from the sides of the pan, it is done. Add the cheese and pour the polenta into a warmed serving bowl. Top with the hot sauce and serve immediately.

Each serving provides:

264	Calories	42 g	Carbohydrate
7 g	Protein	948 mg	Sodium
7 g	Fat	7 mg	Cholesterol
3 g	Dietary Fiber		

Baked Polenta with Cauliflower Sauce and Mozzarella

Here is an earthy and unpretentious dish that is absolutely delicious. Polenta takes some time, and therefore patience, but the technique is simple and you will be happy with the results. A leafy, tart salad and a baked vegetable dish such as Baked Onions with Cream, Nutmeg, and Fresh Mint (page 268) would round out the meal.

Yield: 8 main-course servings

Cauliflower	1	**large (2 pounds)**
Yellow onion	1	**medium, diced**
Celery	2	**inner ribs, diced small**
Garlic	3	**cloves, minced**
Olive oil	1	**tablespoon plus 1 teaspoon**
Dried red chili flakes	¼	**teaspoon**
Tomato puree	2	**cups**
Dried oregano	1	**teaspoon**
Water	8	**cups**
Salt	½	**teaspoon**
Yellow cornmeal	2	**cups**
Parmesan cheese, finely grated	½	**cup**
Part-skim mozzarella, grated	4	**ounces (1 cup)**

Discard the leaves of the cauliflower, then coarsely chop the entire cauliflower, including the core. Heat 1 tablespoon of olive oil in a large skillet or sauté pan over medium heat. Add the onion, celery, garlic, and chili flakes. Stir and sauté 5 minutes. Add the cauliflower, then stir and sauté 5 minutes longer. Add the tomato puree, oregano, and ¼ teaspoon of salt. Reduce heat to medium-low and cook 15–20 minutes, until the cauliflower is tender and breaking apart.

Meanwhile, preheat the oven to 400 degrees F. Use 1 teaspoon of olive oil to rub down a large casserole dish. Bring the water to a boil in a large saucepan with the remaining ¼ teaspoon of salt. Gradually pour in the cornmeal in a slow, steady stream, whisking constantly. Reduce the heat to medium-low and gently simmer about 20 minutes, stirring almost constantly with a wooden spoon. The polenta will thicken as it cooks. When it is thick enough to pull away from the sides of the pan, it is done. Turn off the heat and stir in the Parmesan.

Pour half of the polenta into the casserole dish, top with half of the cauliflower mixture, then sprinkle on half of the mozzarella. Repeat the layers, ending with mozzarella. Bake for 30 minutes and serve hot.

Each serving provides:

268	Calories	42 g	Carbohydrate
12 g	Protein	562 mg	Sodium
7 g	Fat	12 mg	Cholesterol
6 g	Dietary Fiber		

Cannellini Beans with Peppers and Fennel Seed over Parmesan Polenta

Here is a satisfying country supper. In Italy, a plate of grilled sausages might accompany the beans and polenta. For a meatless meal, try grilled baby vegetables and a tart, leafy salad. We relish our polenta enriched by Parmesan cheese; however, you may prefer to use a different variety of cheese, or none at all.

Yield: 6 main-course servings

Olive oil	3	tablespoons
Garlic	4	cloves, minced
Fennel seed	1	teaspoon
Dried red chili flakes	½	teaspoon
Red bell pepper	2	medium, diced
Cooked cannellini beans*	4	cups
Fresh Italian parsley, minced	⅓	cup
Fresh rosemary leaves, minced	1	teaspoon
Salt	½	teaspoon
Bean-cooking liquid or stock	⅔	cup
Dry white wine	⅓	cup
White onion, minced	¾	cup
Italian Vegetable Stock**	6	cups
Yellow cornmeal	1½	cups
Parmesan cheese, finely grated	½	cup

*Cook 1¾ cups of presoaked dried beans for 30–45 minutes (see page 30) until al dente. Alternatively, use canned beans, rinsed and well drained.
**If you do not have any Italian Vegetable Stock on hand, make up a batch using the recipe on page 34, or dissolve 2 large, low-sodium vegetable broth cubes in 6 cups of hot water.

Heat the oil in a large, heavy-bottomed skillet over medium heat. Add the garlic, fennel seed, and chili flakes, and sauté for a moment, then add the red bell pepper and reduce heat to medium-low. Cook, stirring frequently, for 5 minutes. Add the beans, parsley, rosemary, and ¼ teaspoon of salt, and stir to combine, then stir in ⅔ cup of the bean-cooking liquid and the wine (if you do not have bean-cooking liquid on hand, substitute stock or additional wine). Increase the heat to medium-high and cook, stirring gently from time to time, 10 minutes. Most of the liquid will evaporate. Turn off the heat and stir in the onion. Set the beans aside in a warm spot until the polenta is ready.

Meanwhile, bring the stock to a boil with the remaining ¼ teaspoon of salt in a large saucepan over high heat. Gradually pour in the cornmeal in a slow, steady stream, whisking constantly. Reduce the heat to medium-low and gently simmer about 20 minutes, stirring almost constantly with a wooden spoon. The polenta thickens as it cooks. When it is thick enough to pull away from the sides of the pan, it is done. Turn off the heat and stir in the Parmesan.

Distribute the polenta among 6 shallow, warmed bowls. Ladle equal portions of the beans over the polenta and serve hot or warm.

Each serving provides:

436	Calories	67 g	Carbohydrate
18 g	Protein	515 mg	Sodium
10 g	Fat	5 mg	Cholesterol
8 g	Dietary Fiber		

Grilled Polenta Smothered with Sautéed Field Mushrooms

Grilled polenta has become quite popular in restaurants over the past few years. It is easy to prepare and delicious. Guy Hadler perfected this sumptuous dish using a mixture of mushrooms. We like a blend of portobello, shiitake, and crimini with a few button mushrooms thrown in. Several of the preparation steps can be done in advance, if you wish.

Yield: 6 first-course or side-dish servings

The polenta

Water	4	cups
Salt	1	teaspoon
Yellow cornmeal	1	cup
Dried thyme	½	teaspoon
Unsalted butter	2	tablespoons
Parmesan cheese, finely grated	¼	cup

The mushroom sauce

Dried porcini mushrooms	¼	cup
Italian Vegetable Stock*	2	cups
Olive oil	2	tablespoons
Green onions	2,	minced
Fresh Italian parsley, minced	¼	cup
Fresh oregano leaves, minced	1	tablespoon
Fresh rosemary leaves, minced	2	teaspoons
Dry white wine	¾	cup

*If you do not have Italian Vegetable Stock on hand, make some according to the directions on page 34, or dissolve ½ large, low-sodium vegetable broth cube in 2 cups of hot water.

Balsamic vinegar	1	teaspoon
Salt	½	teaspoon
Pepper		Several grinds
Cornstarch	1	tablespoon
Unsalted butter	2	tablespoons
Mixed fresh mushrooms	1	pound
Garlic	2	cloves, minced

Heat the water to a simmer over medium-high heat in a heavy-bottomed saucepan. Crush the thyme with a mortar and pestle to a fine consistency, or crush thoroughly with your fingers, then add to the water along with the salt. Gradually pour in the cornmeal in a slow, steady stream, whisking constantly. Reduce the heat to medium-low and gently simmer about 20 minutes, stirring almost constantly with a wooden spoon. The polenta will thicken as it cooks. When it is thick enough to pull away from the sides of the pan, it is done. Stir in 2 tablespoons of butter and the Parmesan cheese. Pour the hot cooked polenta into a loaf pan, cover with plastic wrap so it does not dry out, and allow it to cool for about 1 hour.

Meanwhile, place the stock in a small saucepan over medium heat and bring to a simmer. Remove from the heat, add the dried porcini mushrooms, cover, and set aside until the mushrooms are tender, about 30 minutes. Clean the fresh mushrooms with a brush or damp cloth and cut them into ¼-inch slices. Set them aside while you complete the sauce.

Reserving the stock, lift out the porcini mushrooms and chop them. Heat 1 tablespoon of olive oil in a medium saucepan at medium-high. Add the chopped porcini mushrooms along with the green onions, parsley, oregano, and rosemary. Sauté for about 2 minutes, stirring occasionally, then add the reserved mushroom-soaking stock and 1 cup of water. Bring to a rapid simmer, cover the pan, and cook over medium for about 10 minutes. Remove the lid and add ½ cup of the wine, the balsamic vinegar, salt, and pepper. Continue to cook over medium-high for about 5 minutes, until the sauce reduces by about half. Strain off the liquid to measure approximately 1½ cups. Discard the onions and herbs. Return the sauce to the pan, but reserve ¼ cup and whisk the cornstarch into it. Heat the sauce over medium-low and whisk in the cornstarch mixture. Cook, stirring occasionally, for 3–5 minutes, until it thickens slightly. (The sauce will not be as thick as a gravy.)

Meanwhile, preheat a coal or gas grill to high, about 500 degrees, then reduce to medium-high. Cut the cooled polenta loaf into slices about ¾-inch thick. Lightly brush or spray the grill with olive oil and place the polenta slices on the grill. Cook 5–6 minutes, then turn and cook the other side.

Meanwhile, heat the remaining 1 tablespoon of olive oil and 2 tablespoons of butter in a large skillet over medium heat. Add the fresh mushrooms and sauté for 5 minutes. Stir in the remaining ¼ cup of wine and the garlic; continue to cook for about 3 minutes. The mushrooms will remain slightly firm. Add the reduced sauce and stir to coat the mushrooms. Place the slices of grilled polenta on a platter or individual plates and top with the mushroom sauce. Serve immediately.

Each serving provides:

280	Calories	32 g	Carbohydrate
5 g	Protein	673 mg	Sodium
14 g	Fat	24 mg	Cholesterol
3 g	Dietary Fiber		

Potato Gnocchi with Sage Gorgonzola Sauce

These melt-in-your-mouth gnocchi combine some of the favorite ingredients of Northern Italians. You will love the pairing of potato and Gorgonzola cheese. This dish can also be served as a first course or side dish for 10, accompanied by grilled fish, salad, and fresh vegetables.

Yield: 6 main-course servings

The gnocchi

Russet potatoes	1	pound (2 medium)
Egg yolk	1	medium
Unbleached flour	½–¾	cup
Salt	½	teaspoon
Pepper		Several grinds

The sauce

Nonfat milk	1½	cups
Unsalted butter	2	tablespoons
Unbleached flour	2	tablespoons
Pepper		Several grinds
Dried sage, crumbled	2	teaspoons
Dry sherry	2	tablespoons
Gorgonzola cheese, crumbled	3	ounces (¾ cup)

Scrub the potatoes and place them in a medium-size saucepan. Cover with water and bring to a boil over high heat. Reduce the heat to medium and cook, uncovered, until very tender, 35–40 minutes. Drain well. Return the potatoes to the pan, and allow to cool and dry out for about 30 minutes. Peel and then mash them or put them through a ricer. Place them in a medium bowl. Lightly beat the egg yolk in a small bowl, then pour it over the potatoes along with the salt and pepper. Mix with a wooden spoon or your hands to completely incorporate. Add ¼ cup of the flour and mix with a wooden spoon or your hands, then add another ¼ cup and mix to incorporate. The resulting dough will be slightly sticky, and begin to form a ball. Transfer the mixture to a lightly floured wooden board, flour your hands, and knead until soft and pliable, 3–5 minutes. Add additional flour if the dough seems too sticky.

Dust a long cutting board or other work surface with flour. Pinch off about ⅙ of the dough at a time and place this small ball on the floured surface. With the flat palm of one hand, use a to-and-fro rolling motion to begin to form a long rope of dough. Use both palms to continue rolling out from the center until the rope is uniformly about ½ inch in diameter. Use a sharp knife to cut the rope into 1-inch-long pieces to form the gnocchi.

For a special touch, use a fingertip to roll each dumpling up along the back of a fork's tines, then let go and allow the dumpling to fall onto the work surface. This produces gnocchi with a fingertip-size indentation on one side and ridges on the other. Line a tray or a baking sheet with a clean, dry tea towel and dust the towel lightly with flour.

Place the finished gnocchi on the tea towel so that they do not touch each other. At this point, they may be refrigerated for several hours or frozen for several months. (Once they are frozen, they may be transferred to a plastic bag.)

To prepare the sauce, heat the milk in a small saucepan over medium-low heat until steaming. Keep hot. Melt the butter in a small skillet over medium-low heat, then stir in the flour, pepper, and sage. Cook for about 1 minute, being careful not to scorch the flour. Add the hot milk in a slow, steady stream, whisking constantly until smoothly incorporated. Add the sherry, and continue to cook for about 5 minutes, until the sauce has thickened. Stir in the cheese and allow it to melt. Keep the sauce warm in a double boiler while you cook the gnocchi.

Meanwhile, bring several quarts of water to a boil in a wide-mouthed pot. Preheat the oven to warm—about 200 degrees F. Place a shallow serving dish in the warm oven. Line another baking sheet with a cotton tea towel and set aside on the counter near the stove. Drop about 12 dumplings at a time into the boiling water. If there are too many in the pot, they may stick to each other. After 1–2 minutes, they will rise to the surface. Continue to cook for about 30 seconds, then remove them with a skimmer, shake off most of the water, and transfer to the towel on the baking sheet to drain. Arrange in a single layer, not touching each other. Place the baking sheet in the warm oven while you cook the remaining gnocchi.

When all the gnocchi are cooked, spoon some of the hot sauce into the warmed serving bowl and add a layer of the gnocchi. Cover with more sauce and the remaining gnocchi. Serve immediately while they are very hot.

Each serving provides:

234	Calories	28 g	Carbohydrate
8 g	Protein	482 mg	Sodium
9 g	Fat	59 mg	Cholesterol
1 g	Dietary Fiber		

Rosemary Potato Gnocchi

Potatoes and rosemary are a classic flavor combination. The simple rosemary-infused butter sauce is highly aromatic.

Yield: 6 main-course servings

The gnocchi

Russet potatoes	1	**pound (2 medium)**
Dried rosemary	1	**teaspoon**
Egg yolk	1	**medium**
Salt	½	**teaspoon**
Pepper		**Several grinds**
Unbleached flour	½–¾	**cup**

The sauce

Unsalted butter	¼	**cup**
Green onions	2,	**minced**
Fresh rosemary, minced	2	**teaspoons**
Parmesan cheese, finely grated	¼	**cup**

Scrub the potatoes and place them in a medium-size saucepan. Cover with water and bring to a boil over high heat. Reduce the heat to medium and cook, uncovered, until very tender, 35–40 minutes. Drain well. Return the potatoes to the pan, and allow to cool and dry out for about 30 minutes. Peel and then mash them or put them through a ricer. Place them in a medium bowl. Lightly beat the egg yolk in a small bowl. Crush the rosemary with a mortar and pestle to a fine consistency, or crush thoroughly with your fingers. Add it to the egg yolk, along with the salt and pepper. Add this to the potatoes and mix with a wooden spoon or your hands to completely incorporate. Add

¼ cup of the flour and mix with a wooden spoon or your hands, then add another ¼ cup and mix to incorporate. The resulting dough will be slightly sticky, and begin to form a ball. Transfer the mixture to a lightly floured wooden board, flour your hands, and knead until soft and pliable, 3–5 minutes. Add additional flour if the dough seems too sticky.

Dust a long cutting board or other work surface with flour. Pinch off about ⅙ of the dough at a time and place this small ball on the floured surface. With the flat palm of one hand, use a to-and-fro rolling motion to begin to form a long rope of dough. Use both palms to continue rolling out from the center until the rope is uniformly about ½ inch in diameter. Use a sharp knife to cut the rope into 1-inch-long pieces to form the gnocchi.

For a special touch, use a fingertip to roll each dumpling up along the back of a fork's tines, then let go and allow the dumpling to fall onto the work surface. This produces a fingertip-size indentation on one side and ridges on the other. Line a tray or a baking sheet with a clean, dry tea towel and dust the towel lightly with flour. Place the finished gnocchi on the tea towel so they do not touch each other. At this point, they may be refrigerated for several hours or frozen for several months. (Once they are frozen, they may be transferred to a plastic bag.)

Meanwhile, bring several quarts of water to a boil in a wide-mouthed pot. Preheat the oven to warm—about 200 degrees F. Place a shallow serving dish in the warm oven and line another baking sheet with a cotton tea towel. Drop about 12 dumplings at a time into the boiling water. If there are too many in the pot, they may stick to each other. After 1–2 minutes, they will rise to the surface. Allow them to continue to cook for about 30 seconds, then remove them with a skimmer or small sieve, shake off most of the water, and transfer to the towel on the baking sheet to drain. Arrange in a single layer, not touching each other. Keep the baking sheet in the warm oven while you cook the remaining gnocchi.

When the gnocchi are cooked, prepare the sauce. In a sauté pan, melt the butter over medium-low heat. Add the green onions and rosemary and sauté for 2 minutes. Add the cooked gnocchi to the pan and stir gently for about 1 minute to coat. Transfer to a warmed serving dish, using a rubber spatula to scrape all the butter and onions out of the pan. Toss with the Parmesan and serve.

Each serving provides:

200	Calories	23 g	Carbohydrate
4 g	Protein	257 mg	Sodium
10 g	Fat	59 mg	Cholesterol
2 g	Dietary Fiber		

Spinach Ricotta Gnocchi
with Herbed Tomato Coulis

Gnocchi is admittedly a bit time-consuming to prepare, but it is such fun! If you enlist the aid of family members or friends, the task of shaping the gnocchi becomes an enjoyable way to spend time together. And you get to eat the delicious results. This wonderful variation on the gnocchi theme is made with ricotta cheese and without potato. Use any Italian herbs growing in your garden—oregano, marjoram, and thyme is a good combination.

Yield: 6 main-course servings

The gnocchi

Part-skim ricotta cheese	1½ cups
Romano cheese, finely grated	¼ cup
Cooked spinach, fresh or frozen, chopped	½ cup
Egg	1 large
Salt	½ teaspoon
Unbleached flour	1½ cups plus 6 tablespoons

The sauce

Fresh pear tomatoes	2½ pounds
Olive oil	1 tablespoon
Garlic	2 cloves, minced
Fresh mixed herbs (your choice), minced	2 tablespoons
Salt	⅛ teaspoon
Pepper	Several grinds
Dry red wine	⅓ cup

In a bowl, stir together the ricotta and Romano cheeses, spinach, egg, and salt until well combined. Stir in 1 cup of the flour until too thick to stir, then use your hands to mix in another ½ cup of flour. Transfer the dough to a lightly floured board and knead about 2–3 minutes, adding additional flour 1 tablespoon at a time if the dough is too sticky.

Dust a long cutting board or other work surface with flour. Pinch off about ⅙ of the dough at a time and place this small ball on the floured surface. With the flat palm of one hand, use a to-and-fro rolling motion to begin to form a long rope of dough. Use both palms to continue rolling out from the center until the rope is uniformly about ½ inch in diameter. Use a sharp knife to cut the rope into 1-inch-long pieces to form the gnocchi.

For a special touch, use a fingertip to roll each dumpling up along the back of a fork's tines, then let go and allow the dumpling to fall onto the work surface. This produces gnocchi with a fingertip-size indentation on one side and ridges on the other. Line a tray or baking sheet with a clean, dry tea towel and dust the towel lightly with flour. Place the finished gnocchi on the tea towel so they do not touch each other. At this point, they may be refrigerated for several hours or frozen for several months. (Once they are frozen, they may be transferred to a plastic bag.)

Meanwhile, heat several quarts of water in a large stockpot. When it is steaming, drop in the pear tomatoes and allow to heat for about 2 minutes, until some of the skins have split. Remove the tomatoes to a bowl to cool slightly. (Save the water to boil the gnocchi in.) When the tomatoes are cool enough to handle, peel them. Squeeze each tomato gently to remove the seeds and most of the juice. (The juice can be saved for another use, such as soup.)

Heat the olive oil in a skillet at a medium setting. Add the garlic and herbs, and cook until sizzling—only about 1 minute. Excessive browning will turn the garlic bitter. Add the tomatoes, draining off any juice that has collected, and stir in the salt, pepper, and wine. Continue to cook over medium heat about 10 minutes, until the tomatoes are thoroughly cooked. Transfer to a blender or food processor and puree. Return the sauce to the skillet and keep it warm.

Meanwhile, bring the water used for the tomatoes to a boil in a wide-mouthed pot. Preheat the oven to warm—about 200 degrees F. Place a shallow serving bowl in the warm oven and line another baking sheet with a cotton tea towel. Drop about 12 dumplings at a time into the boiling water. If there are too many in the pot, they may stick to each other. After 1–2 minutes, they will rise to the surface. Allow them to continue to cook for about 30 seconds, then remove them with a skimmer or small sieve, shake off as much water as possible, and transfer to the towel on the baking sheet to drain. Arrange in a single layer, not touching each other. Place the baking sheet in the warm oven while you cook the remaining dumplings.

Add the cooked gnocchi to the finished sauce in the skillet, and stir to distribute the sauce evenly. Transfer to the warmed bowl and serve immediately, passing additional Romano cheese, if desired.

Each serving provides:

325	Calories	43 g	Carbohydrate
16 g	Protein	403 mg	Sodium
10 g	Fat	58 mg	Cholesterol
4 g	Dietary Fiber		

Hot Vegetable Dishes

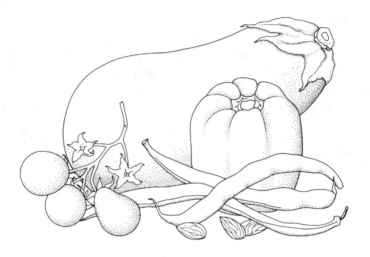

Many of the best-known vegetables in the United States were originally cultivated in Italy. Broccoli and zucchini, two of America's favorites, still carry their Italian names.

    Italians are serious about the quality of their vegetables. Nearly every household plants a garden in whatever spot of ground is available, and most of the country's fresh food is still produced on small family farms in the countryside. Almost all Italian cities, towns, and villages boast a lively and colorful daily outdoor market, where food lovers convene to select the very best produce the growers have to offer. Cooks mark the change of seasons by watching for the first green peas of spring or the vine-ripened red tomatoes of summer to appear at their favorite market stalls.

Italian cooks treat vegetables with imagination and respect, even if the preparation is as simple as a quick pan sauté. Fruity olive oil, fresh herbs, aged cheese, and fine wine are among their most treasured seasonings, always used in quantities and combinations that enhance the natural goodness of the chosen vegetable.

In addition to their place in an infinite variety of antipasti and salads, vegetables appear on Italian tables as *contorno*, an accompaniment to the main course. We have included a tempting selection of such side dishes in this chapter, along with a few vegetable creations hearty and impressive enough to be the center of the meal.

Tips and Tools

- Most vegetables taste best when cooked to the al dente stage, retaining some firmness but easy to pierce with a fork. Overcooking renders them unappetizing, so test frequently and serve vegetables barely tender for best results.

- Certain cut vegetables, such as artichokes, should be kept in acidulated (slightly acid) water to prevent oxidation, which causes darkening. Acidulate water by combining about 2 quarts of cold water with about 6 tablespoons of lemon juice or vinegar in a large bowl.

- A collapsible streaming tray, made of perforated stainless steel, is a valuable aid in vegetable cooking. You will also need a pot with a tight-fitting lid for vegetable steaming.

Green Beans with Garlic and Parmesan

ALMOST INSTANT

This dish is the epitome of Italian cooking—fast, simple, and fresh. Begin with the freshest green beans you can find, and be sure not to overcook them. Try this same preparation substituting almost any fresh, in-season vegetable.

Yield: 6 side-dish servings

Green beans	1	**pound**
Olive oil	1	**tablespoon**
Garlic	2	**cloves, minced**
Salt	⅛	**teaspoon**
Pepper		**Several grinds**
Parmesan cheese, finely grated	2	**tablespoons**

Trim the beans and cut them into 1-inch lengths. Place the beans on a steamer rack in a saucepan that has a tight-fitting lid. Add about 1 inch of water, cover, and cook over medium-high heat 8–10 minutes, until fork-tender. Meanwhile, place the olive oil in a small pan over low heat. Add the garlic, salt, and pepper; sauté for 1–2 minutes. You want to cook—but not brown—the garlic. Remove the pan from the heat. Transfer the cooked beans to a warmed serving bowl and drizzle with the oil-garlic mixture. Toss to combine. Sprinkle with the Parmesan cheese, toss again, and serve.

Each serving provides:

49	Calories	5 g	Carbohydrate
2 g	Protein	75 mg	Sodium
3 g	Fat	1 mg	Cholesterol
1 g	Dietary Fiber		

Zucchini with Browned Butter and Garlic

ALMOST INSTANT

Here is a quick, simple, and classic way to prepare zucchini. It works just as well with many other vegetables, including broccoli, green beans, and carrots. Select firm, unblemished zucchini for best results.

Yield: 4 side-dish servings

Zucchini	1	**pound (3 medium)**
Unsalted butter	2	**tablespoons**
Garlic	2	**cloves, minced**
Salt		**A pinch**
Pepper		**Several grinds**

Wash and dry the zucchini. Trim off the ends and cut each squash in half lengthwise. Cut the halves crosswise into ½-inch chunks. Place on a steamer tray in a pan with a tight-fitting lid. Add 1–2 inches of warm water to the pan. Cover and cook over medium-high heat until zucchini pieces are very tender but not falling apart (cooking time depends on the thickness of the zucchini; 8–12 minutes is average). When the zucchini are nearly done, place the butter in a skillet over medium heat. When it has melted and is just beginning to brown, tilt the pan back and forth and cook no more than 1 minute longer. The idea is to thoroughly brown the butter without burning it. Immediately remove the skillet from the heat and stir in the garlic. The zucchini should be done at the same time. If they aren't, set the butter aside and reheat briefly before tossing with the well-drained zucchini, salt, and pepper in a warmed serving bowl. Serve hot.

Each serving provides:

73	Calories	4 g	Carbohydrate
2 g	Protein	34 mg	Sodium
6 g	Fat	16 mg	Cholesterol
1 g	Dietary Fiber		

Marsala Glazed Carrots

These delectable carrots make a nice presentation and are simple to prepare. Use carrots no more than half an inch in diameter so they will cook properly in the allotted time.

Yield: 4 side-dish servings

Baby carrots	**¾**	**pound**
Unsalted butter	**2**	**tablespoons**
Marsala	**¾**	**cup**
Fresh Italian parsley, minced	**2**	**tablespoons**
Fresh lemon wedges	**1**	**per serving**

Wash the carrots well but don't peel them. Melt the butter in a heavy-bottomed sauté pan over medium heat. Add the whole carrots in a single layer. Sauté for 10 minutes, shaking the pan frequently so carrots brown evenly. Add the Marsala and cook for about 10 minutes longer, until carrots are tender and Marsala has reduced to a few tablespoons of syrupy liquid. Transfer the carrots to a warmed serving plate and drizzle with the Marsala syrup. Sprinkle with the parsley and garnish the plate with lemon wedges, to be squeezed over the carrots by each diner, if desired.

Each serving provides:

125	Calories	12 g	Carbohydrate
1 g	Protein	61 mg	Sodium
6 g	Fat	16 mg	Cholesterol
1 g	Dietary Fiber		

Broccoli Sautéed with Garlic and Olives

ALMOST INSTANT, VEGAN

Broccoli is an eminently popular vegetable, delicious when lightly steamed, and fabulous when prepared with an Italian flair. Dry oil-cured black olives from Southern Italy are perfect for this dish, but if they are unavailable, you may substitute Greek Kalamata olives.

Yield: 6 side-dish servings

Broccoli	1½	**pounds**
Olive oil	2	**tablespoons**
Marsala	2	**tablespoons**
Garlic	4	**cloves, minced**
Dry oil-cured black olives	¼	**cup**
Pepper		**Several grinds**

Trim off and discard the tough ends of the broccoli stems. Coarsely chop the remaining stem portions and the florets. Heat the olive oil and Marsala in a large skillet over medium heat and add the garlic. Sauté for about 2 minutes, then add the broccoli, ½ cup of water, and the pepper. Cover and cook for 12 minutes, stirring occasionally. If the liquid is gone but the broccoli is not yet tender, add one or two tablespoons of water and replace the lid. Stir in the olives during the last 2 minutes of the cooking time. Serve immediately.

Each serving provides:

76	Calories	6 g	Carbohydrate
3 g	Protein	41 mg	Sodium
5 g	Fat	0 mg	Cholesterol
3 g	Dietary Fiber		

Sautéed Spinach with Sherry, Cinnamon, Raisins, and Pine Nuts

ALMOST INSTANT, VEGAN

This recipe brings together some favorite flavors of old Rome, where sweet and savory seasonings were combined in ways that seem unconventional to most Americans. This wonderful dish is simple to prepare, once you have taken the time to clean the spinach properly.

Yield: 4 side-dish servings

Fresh spinach	**3**	**pounds**
Pine nuts	**2**	**tablespoons**
Extra virgin olive oil	**1**	**tablespoon**
Ground cinnamon	**⅛**	**teaspoon**
Garlic	**2**	**cloves, minced**
Golden raisins, minced	**3**	**tablespoons**
Dry sherry	**2**	**tablespoons**
Salt		**A pinch**
Pepper		**Several grinds**

Carefully clean the spinach and discard the stems. Pile the wet leaves into a large pot, cover, and cook over medium heat 5–8 minutes, until uniformly wilted, stirring once halfway through. Transfer the spinach to a colander to drain, pressing with the back of a wooden spoon to remove a good deal, but not all, of the water. You want it to be moist but not dripping wet. (You may want to collect the spinach juices in a bowl to use in your next soup stock.) When cool enough to handle, finely chop the spinach and set aside.

Meanwhile, toast the pine nuts (see page 31) and chop finely. Set aside. Heat the olive oil in a large skillet and add the cinnamon and garlic. When sizzling, add the raisins and sherry, stir for about 1 minute, then add the spinach, salt, and pepper, and stir well to combine the ingredients. Gently pat the spinach down into an even, thin layer on the bottom of the pan, reduce heat to low, and cook for 3–4 minutes, until spinach is steaming hot. Spinach should appear moist, but all liquid in the bottom of the pan should have evaporated. If necessary, increase the heat a little and cook off any excess liquid. Transfer the hot spinach to a warmed serving dish and sprinkle evenly with the pine nuts. Serve hot or at room temperature.

Each serving provides:

158	Calories	19 g	Carbohydrate
11 g	Protein	295 mg	Sodium
7 g	Fat	0 mg	Cholesterol
9 g	Dietary Fiber		

Braised Broccoli Rabe and Swiss Chard with Sherry

ALMOST INSTANT, VEGAN

Broccoli rabe is a wild form of the commercial broccoli with which Americans are more familiar. Known as cime di rapa *or* rapini *in Italy, and sometimes sold as broccoli rape in American markets, this vegetable is prized for its sharp bitterness. It is available from fall through early spring in most Italian markets and many local produce stands. In this dish, the chard and seasonings act as a delightful counterpoint to the broccoli rabe.*

Yield: 6 side-dish servings

Broccoli rabe	¾	**pound**
Swiss chard	¾	**pound**
Fresh-squeezed lemon juice	¼	**cup**
Dry sherry	2	**tablespoons**
Extra virgin olive oil	1	**tablespoon**
Dried red chili flakes	¼	**teaspoon**

Wash the broccoli rabe and the chard, but do not dry them. Coarsely chop them. Place the oil, lemon juice, sherry, and 2 tablespoons of water in a large pan that has a tight-fitting lid. Crush the chili flakes with a mortar and pestle, and add them to the pot. Pile in the vegetables, tossing to coat with the lemon juice mixture. Cover the pot and cook over medium-high heat for 10 minutes, until the vegetables wilt. Stir once halfway through the cooking time. Transfer to a warmed bowl and serve immediately.

Each serving provides:

50	Calories	6 g	Carbohydrate
3 g	Protein	129 mg	Sodium
2 g	Fat	0 mg	Cholesterol
3 g	Dietary Fiber		

Artichokes Braised with Parsley and Lemon

VEGAN

We first ate artichokes prepared this way in the town square of Siena, the beautiful Gothic city in Tuscany. They melted in our mouths and satisfied our taste buds as much as the scenery excited our minds. This recipe works best with medium-size artichokes. The preparation might seem wasteful, as the outer leaves of the artichokes are removed before cooking and only the tender inner leaves and bottoms are eaten. However, the outer leaves need not be discarded; you can steam them separately and eat them in the conventional American way with mayonnaise. Or consider making the delightful pasta side dish called Farfalle with Artichoke Pesto and Mascarpone (page 154), which calls for the precise amount of pulp yielded from scraping the leaves of 4 medium artichokes.

Yield: 8 side-dish servings

Artichokes	**4**	**medium (2 pounds)**
Extra virgin olive oil	**¼**	**cup**
Fresh-squeezed lemon juice	**⅓**	**cup**
Garlic	**5**	**cloves, minced**
Dried red chili flakes	**¼**	**teaspoon**
Salt	**¼**	**teaspoon**
Pepper		**Several grinds**
Fresh Italian parsley, minced	**½**	**cup**

Prepare acidulated water in a large bowl by combining 2 quarts of cold water with 6 tablespoons of lemon juice or vinegar. Set aside near your work surface.

Trim the artichokes, working with 1 artichoke at a time. Use your hands to snap off all the tough outer leaves until you get down to the pale leaves at the center. Use a sharp knife to cut off the leaf tips, leaving only the base and yellowish green leaves. Cut off ¼ inch of the stem end, then peel the stem and the bottom of each artichoke. Proceed until you have trimmed all the artichokes in this manner, dropping each artichoke into the acidulated water as you finish. Next, remove the artichoke hearts from the water one at a time and quarter them from stem to top. Use a paring knife or melon baller to scrape out the fuzzy "choke" portion. Finally, slice each quarter lengthwise into thirds or fourths, depending on their size. You want wedges about ¼-inch thick. As you go, drop the artichoke pieces back into the acidulated water.

Heat the olive oil over medium in a large skillet that has a tight-fitting lid. Add ½ cup of fresh water, the lemon juice, dried chili flakes, garlic, salt, and pepper. Remove the artichoke pieces from the acidulated water and drain them briefly on a kitchen towel. Add them to the pan, toss to coat, cover, and cook 15–20 minutes, until barely fork-tender, stirring at the halfway point. Check frequently toward the end of the cooking time as the liquid will almost be cooked away. If the liquid evaporates before the artichokes are done, add 1–2 tablespoons of water and continue to cook. Remove from the heat, add the parsley, toss, and transfer to a serving dish. Serve hot or at room temperature.

Each serving provides:

96	Calories	8 g	Carbohydrate
2 g	Protein	125 mg	Sodium
7 g	Fat	0 mg	Cholesterol
3 g	Dietary Fiber		

Braised Turnips with Chives and Parsley

ALMOST INSTANT, VEGAN

Unfortunately, turnips seem to have a bad reputation. In reality, they are nourishing—and delicious when properly cooked. In many regions of Italy, they are favored by the country people, who know how to make the most of simple ingredients. Rutabaga or kohlrabi can also be cooked as described in this recipe, and other herbs can be substituted for the parsley and chives, if you prefer.

Yield: 4 side-dish servings

Turnips	1	**pound**
Olive oil	1½	**tablespoons**
Salt	¼	**teaspoon**
Pepper		**Several grinds**
Italian Vegetable Stock or dry white wine	⅓	**cup**
Fresh chives, minced	3	**tablespoons**
Fresh Italian parsley, minced	3	**tablespoons, lightly packed**

Peel the turnips and chop them into roughly ½-inch cubes. Heat the oil in a skillet over medium-high heat and add the turnips. Sauté about 10 minutes, stirring frequently, until they are browning nicely. Stir in the salt and pepper, then add the stock and immediately cover the pan tightly. Reduce heat to medium-low and cook 10 minutes. Remove the lid and continue to stir and sauté until all the liquid has evaporated and the turnips are tender, about 3–5 minutes. Stir in the chives and parsley, and transfer to a serving dish. Serve hot or warm.

Each serving provides:

79	Calories	7 g	Carbohydrate
1 g	Protein	226 mg	Sodium
5 g	Fat	0 mg	Cholesterol
2 g	Dietary Fiber		

Braised Chard with Tomatoes and Olives

ALMOST INSTANT, VEGAN

Chard is an often overlooked vegetable, yet so tasty and easy to prepare. In Southern Italy and especially Sicily, chard is very popular. This side dish combines it with tomatoes and olives, also native to the south.

Yield: 6 side-dish servings

Swiss chard	1½	pounds (about 2 bunches)
Olive oil	1	tablespoon
Garlic	3	cloves, minced
Pear tomatoes	1	14.5-ounce can
Salt	¼	teaspoon
Pepper		Several grinds
Dry oil-cured black olives, pitted and chopped	⅓	cup

Immerse the chard in a large basin of cold water. Carefully wash the chard leaves but do not dry them; water should still cling to the leaves. Coarsely chop, removing the stem ends if they are tough. Place the oil in a large, heavy-bottomed pan that has a tight-fitting lid. Heat over medium and add the garlic. Sauté for about 1 minute, but do not brown. Add the tomatoes along with their juice. Use a metal spoon or a knife to coarsely chop the tomatoes, then add the salt and pepper. Pile in the chard, stir briefly, and cover. Cook for about 20 minutes. Stir halfway through the cooking time to bring some of the tomatoes to the top. Add the olives, stir to incorporate, and serve.

Each serving provides:

76	Calories	8 g	Carbohydrate
2 g	Protein	658 mg	Sodium
5 g	Fat	0 mg	Cholesterol
1 g	Dietary Fiber		

Grilled Eggplant with Basil Pesto and Fresh Tomatoes

Cooking outdoors is the perfect way to prepare eggplant during the summer, its peak season. The grill lends a slightly smoky flavor in this fantasia dish that is a distant cousin of traditional eggplant parmigiana. Here, each slice stands alone, not immersed in sauce. Serve this side dish with grilled fish and salad for a lovely meal. The Basil Pesto may be homemade or commercially prepared.

Yield: 8 side-dish servings

Eggplant	1	**pound (1 medium)**
Olive oil	2	**tablespoons**
Basil Pesto (see page 134)	⅓	**cup**
Parmesan cheese, finely grated	¼	**cup**
Part-skim mozzarella	4	**ounces**
Fresh pear tomatoes	½	**pound (3 medium)**
Fresh basil leaves	10	**large**

Preheat a coal or gas grill to medium-high. Without peeling, cut the eggplant crosswise into ½-inch-thick slices. Coat your hands with some of the oil, then gently oil each slice of eggplant. Place the slices on the grill, cover the grill, and cook for about 10 minutes, until slightly charred and beginning to soften. Turn and continue to cook for 5 minutes. Cut the mozzarella and tomatoes into thin slices. Open the grill and top each slice of eggplant with some mozzarella. Spoon on the Basil Pesto then top each eggplant slice with a tomato slice, a sprinkle of Parmesan, and a basil leaf. Cover the grill and cook for 5 more minutes. Serve immediately.

Each serving provides:

153	Calories	6 g	Carbohydrate
6 g	Protein	148 mg	Sodium
12 g	Fat	12 mg	Cholesterol
1 g	Dietary Fiber		

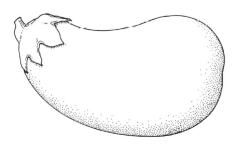

Asparagus with Watercress and Green Onion Sauce

ALMOST INSTANT

Asparagus and watercress both appear in the spring. This dish combines them beautifully. Like the Italians, we enjoy fresh asparagus as often as we can during its short season.

Yield: 8 side-dish servings

Egg	1	medium
Fresh asparagus	2	pounds
Watercress leaves	½	cup
Green onions	2,	chopped
Olive oil	3	tablespoons
Fresh-squeezed lemon juice	2	tablespoons
Salt	⅛	teaspoon
Pepper		Several grinds

Hard-boil the egg and cool in a pan of cold water. Peel, finely chop, and set aside.

Meanwhile, wash the asparagus carefully to remove any traces of soil. Snap off the tough ends. Place on a steamer rack in a pan with a tight-fitting lid. Add 2 inches of water to the pan and cook over medium-high until just fork-tender, about 6 minutes, depending on the thickness of the stems. Be careful not to overcook—when in doubt, it is better to err on the undercooked side.

Combine the oil, lemon juice, salt, and pepper in a small bowl. Place the watercress and onions in a blender. Switch on the low setting and add the oil and lemon juice mixture in a slow, steady stream. The resulting sauce will be a bright springtime green. Arrange the cooked asparagus on a serving platter and top with the sauce. Sprinkle on the chopped egg and serve hot or at room temperature.

Each serving provides:

75	Calories	4 g	Carbohydrate
3 g	Protein	48 mg	Sodium
6 g	Fat	28 mg	Cholesterol
1 g	Dietary Fiber		

Cauliflower al Gratine with Fresh Parsley and Oregano

ALMOST INSTANT

Fresh foods, simply prepared, are the heart of Italian cuisine. This cauliflower dish highlights the ingredients that would be found in a Sicilian garden in late winter and early spring. If you do not have a garden, prepare it anytime the cauliflower at the market looks good.

Yield: 6 side-dish servings

Cauliflower	2½	**pounds**
Garlic	4	**cloves, minced**
Fresh oregano leaves, minced	2	**tablespoons**
Fresh Italian parsley, minced	1	**tablespoon**
Coarse dry bread crumbs	½	**cup**
Unsalted butter	2	**tablespoons, melted**
Parmesan cheese, finely grated	2	**tablespoons**

Preheat the oven to 350 degrees F. Trim off and discard the leaves of the cauliflower and chop it into florets. Place the florets on a steamer rack in a large saucepan that has a tight-fitting lid. Add about 2 inches of water, cover the pan, and cook over medium-high heat about 10 minutes, until just fork-tender. Drain into a colander and rinse with cold water to stop the cooking.

Butter a 2½-quart baking dish and add the cauliflower. Evenly distribute the chopped garlic, oregano, and parsley over it. Top evenly with the bread crumbs, then drizzle on the melted butter. Sprinkle with the Parmesan cheese to lightly cover. Bake, uncovered, for about 12 minutes, until golden brown on top. Serve immediately.

Each serving provides:

120	Calories	15 g	Carbohydrate
5 g	Protein	115 mg	Sodium
5 g	Fat	12 mg	Cholesterol
4 g	Dietary Fiber		

Roasted Tomatoes al Gratine

VEGAN

This simple summer dish is great with a creamy pasta or risotto. Commercial bread crumbs are fine, although it is easy and economical to turn stale bread into homemade bread crumbs (see page 32).

Yield: 6 side-dish servings

Fresh pear tomatoes	1	**pound (6 medium)**
Yellow onion	½	**medium, chopped**
Garlic	1	**clove, minced**
Fresh Italian parsley, minced	2	**tablespoons**
Fresh rosemary leaves, minced	1	**teaspoon**
Salt	¼	**teaspoon**
Pepper		**Several grinds**
Extra virgin olive oil	1	**tablespoon plus ¼ teaspoon**
Coarse dry bread crumbs	2	**tablespoons**

Preheat the oven to 350 degrees F. Lightly oil a 1½-quart glass baking dish with ¼ teaspoon of oil. Cut the tomatoes in half lengthwise and place them cut side up in the dish. Mix together the onion, garlic, parsley, rosemary, salt, and pepper. Evenly distribute this mixture over the tomatoes. Drizzle with 1 tablespoon of olive oil and top with the bread crumbs. Bake, uncovered, for 45 minutes.

Each serving provides:

54	Calories	7 g	Carbohydrate
1 g	Protein	110 mg	Sodium
3 g	Fat	0 mg	Cholesterol
1 g	Dietary Fiber		

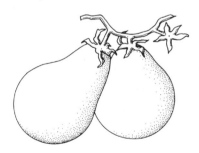

Mushrooms al Gratine with Lemon Thyme Cream Sauce

Decidedly rich and filling, this wonderful mushroom preparation is delicious served alongside any light main course or as an antipasto atop crostini. If you can find fresh field mushrooms, such as porcini or chanterelles, substitute them for some of the button mushrooms to create an extra-special dish.

Yield: 6 side-dish servings

Mushrooms	1½	**pounds**
Lowfat milk	1½	**cups**
Unsalted butter	2	**tablespoons plus 1 teaspoon**
Garlic	1	**clove, minced**
Unbleached flour	1½	**tablespoons**
Dried thyme	¼	**teaspoon**
Freshly grated nutmeg	¼	**teaspoon**
Salt	⅛	**teaspoon**
Pepper		**Several grinds**
Fresh-squeezed lemon juice	1	**tablespoon**
Parmesan cheese, finely grated	2	**tablespoons**

Preheat the oven to 375 degrees F. Rub an 8 × 8-inch baking dish or individual au gratin dishes with ½ teaspoon of butter. Clean the mushrooms with a brush or damp cloth and quarter them to create wedges. Pour the milk into a small saucepan and set aside.

Melt 1 tablespoon of the butter over medium-high heat. Before it browns, add the mushrooms and quickly stir to coat with butter. Sauté about 5 minutes, stirring occasionally, until mushrooms begin to brown and release a little of their juice. Use a slotted spoon to transfer the mushrooms to the buttered baking dish, creating an even layer. Set aside. Use a rubber spatula to scrape the mushroom pan juices into the milk in the saucepan. Heat this mixture over low until it is steaming. Do not allow it to boil.

Melt the remaining 1 tablespoon of butter in the same pan used to sauté the mushrooms. Stir in the garlic, then immediately add the flour. Stir as the flour absorbs the butter and cooks for about 1 minute, then add half of the hot milk and whisk to incorporate. When the sauce has thickened a bit, add the remaining milk, thyme, nutmeg, salt, and pepper. Cook over medium heat, stirring frequently, until quite thick, about 7 minutes. Stir in the lemon juice and pour the sauce over the mushrooms. Top evenly with the Parmesan. Bake about 20 minutes, until sauce is bubbling and Parmesan has browned slightly. Serve hot.

Each serving provides:

119	Calories	11 g	Carbohydrate
5 g	Protein	122 mg	Sodium
7 g	Fat	19 mg	Cholesterol
2 g	Dietary Fiber		

Roasted Vegetables with Orange Balsamic Glaze

VEGAN

This dish calls for slender baby carrots, tiny red or white potatoes, and mild shallots. Yet any combination of vegetables can be cooked this way. Add strips of bell pepper or try parsnips, turnips, or sweet potatoes for variety. Except for your careful attention at the last minute, this dish is trouble-free. Simply pop it in the oven and go about your business.

Yield: 6 side-dish servings

Baby carrots	½	**pound**
Fresh shallots	½	**pound**
Small red or white potatoes	1	**pound**
Extra virgin olive oil	1½	**tablespoons**
Salt	⅛	**teaspoon**
Pepper		**Several grinds**
Fresh-squeezed orange juice	3	**tablespoons**
Balsamic vinegar	3	**tablespoons**

Preheat the oven to 375 degrees F. Wash the carrots and blot them dry. If they are long, cut them at a slant crosswise into 2-inch-long pieces. Put them in a large bowl. Peel the shallots and, if they are large, separate them into individual cloves. Add to the carrots in the bowl. Rinse the potatoes, or scrub them if they are dirty. If they are larger than 1½ inches in diameter, cut them in halves or quarters to achieve that size. Add the potatoes to the bowl. Pour the olive oil over the vegetables and toss with a wooden spoon until they are evenly coated. Add the salt and pepper, and toss again. Transfer the vegetables to a large covered casserole or baking dish that can tolerate the direct flame of the stove top once the baking is done. Cover and bake 45 minutes to 1 hour, until the largest vegetable pieces are fork-tender. Transfer the vegetables from the baking dish to a pretty serving plate and set aside in a warm place.

Place the baking dish on the stove over medium heat and stir in the orange juice and vinegar. Bring to a simmer and cook, stirring almost constantly, about 7 minutes, until liquid has reduced by about half to form a slightly thick sauce. Drizzle this sauce over the vegetables and serve warm or at room temperature.

Each serving provides:

165	Calories	32 g	Carbohydrate
3 g	Protein	79 mg	Sodium
4 g	Fat	0 mg	Cholesterol
2 g	Dietary Fiber		

Baked Onions with Cream, Nutmeg, and Fresh Mint

Select the firmest, smallest onions you can find for this recipe—any color will do. It is a wonderful dish to serve alongside a baked main course such as Baked Polenta with Cauliflower Sauce and Mozzarella (page 222). The bright, piquant flavor of mint makes this dish a masterpiece.

Yield: 4 side-dish servings

Small onions	1	**pound**
Italian Vegetable Stock*	1	**cup**
Unsalted butter	1	**tablespoon**
Salt	⅛	**teaspoon**
Pepper		**Several grinds**
Heavy cream	2	**tablespoons**
Fresh mint leaves, minced	3	**tablespoons**
Freshly grated nutmeg		**To taste**

Preheat the oven to 400 degrees F. Peel the onions and cut into pieces about 1½ inches in their largest dimension. Pearl onions may be left whole. Meanwhile, heat the stock until steaming in a small saucepan. Place the onions in an 8 × 8-inch baking dish or oval casserole and pour the hot stock over them. Cover the dish and bake for 20–25 minutes, until they are fork-tender. Use a slotted spoon to transfer the onions to a pretty serving dish; turn off the oven and place the dish inside to keep warm.

*If you do not have Italian Vegetable Stock on hand, make some according to the directions on page 34, or dissolve ½ of a large, low-sodium vegetable broth cube in 1 cup of hot water.

Bring ½ cup of the onion-cooking liquid to a simmer in a small saucepan or skillet over medium heat. Add the butter, salt, and pepper, and allow to simmer rapidly for 3–4 minutes, until liquid reduces to about ¼ cup. Add the cream and stir constantly as you cook another 3–4 minutes, until sauce has a slightly thick consistency.

Discard any watery liquid that has accumulated in the bottom of the dish that holds the onions. Pour the sauce evenly over the onions, dust with the nutmeg, and top with the mint. Serve hot.

Each serving provides:

92	Calories	9 g	Carbohydrate
1 g	Protein	392 mg	Sodium
6 g	Fat	19 mg	Cholesterol
1 g	Dietary Fiber		

Eggplant Parmigiana
with Fresh Oregano

There are many variations on this classic Italian dish. Ours is light-
ened up by broiling the eggplant, rather than breading and frying it.
If your broiler pan is well tempered, no oil should be required. The
texture of this rich, satisfying casserole is almost soufflélike. Fresh
oregano adds a bright note to the flavor. A simple side dish such as
Broccoli Sautéed with Garlic and Olives (page 245) makes a wonder-
ful accompaniment, along with a tart salad and good crusty bread.

Yield: 4 main-course servings

Eggplants	2	medium (2 pounds)
Coarse dry bread crumbs	1	cup
Fresh Italian parsley, minced	½	cup
Fresh pear tomatoes	2½	pounds
Olive oil	1	tablespoon plus 1 teaspoon
Garlic	4	cloves, minced
Salt	¼	teaspoon
Pepper		Several grinds
Dry white wine	⅓	cup
Fresh oregano leaves, minced	2	tablespoons
Parmesan cheese, finely grated	1	cup

Preheat the broiler. Wash and dry the eggplants and cut them
crosswise into ¼-inch-thick slices. Place on the broiler pan
about 4 inches under the broiler until the surface of the eggplant
is well browned, about 5 minutes. Turn the slices over and broil
another 5 minutes. Eggplant slices should be fairly limp but not
falling apart. (Alternatively, you may grill the eggplant slices
until tender and nicely browned.)

Meanwhile, cut the tomatoes in half crosswise and gently squeeze out the seed pockets. Chop the tomatoes coarsely and set aside. Heat 1 tablespoon of olive oil in a sauté pan over medium heat and sauté the garlic for about 1 minute. Add the chopped tomatoes, salt, and pepper, and cook over medium heat, stirring frequently, until tomatoes are softening and have released their liquid, about 10 minutes. Stir in the wine and oregano, and cook another 3 minutes.

Preheat the oven to 375 degrees F. Toss the bread crumbs with the parsley and set aside. Use 1 teaspoon of olive oil to rub down a 2-quart casserole dish. Arrange half of the eggplant slices in an even layer on the bottom of the dish. Top evenly with half of the bread crumb mixture. Top the crumbs evenly with half of the tomato sauce. Top with half of the Parmesan. Repeat the layers, ending with Parmesan. Bake for 30 minutes, until the top of the casserole is nicely browned.

Each serving provides:

368	Calories	48 g	Carbohydrate
17 g	Protein	738 mg	Sodium
13 g	Fat	17 mg	Cholesterol
7 g	Dietary Fiber		

Stuffed Eggplants with Tomatoes, Capers, and Oregano

Some classic flavors of Southern Italy come together in this very special eggplant main dish. While it is baking, you can put together a simple pasta first course and a light salad to follow the main course. A briefly steamed green vegetable, such as green beans or broccoli spears, topped with Garlic Maionese (page 136) and minced red onion, looks appealing on the plate alongside the eggplants and offers some textural contrast.

Yield: 4 main-course servings

Eggplants	2	**pounds (2 medium)**
Olive oil	2	**teaspoons**
Parmesan cheese, finely grated	¼	**cup plus 2 tablespoons**
Canned chopped tomatoes	1	**cup**
Part-skim ricotta cheese	¾	**cup**
Coarse dry bread crumbs	½	**cup**
Capers, rinsed and drained	2	**tablespoons, minced**
Fresh oregano leaves	2	**tablespoons, minced**
Garlic	3	**cloves, minced**
Salt	½	**teaspoon**
Pepper		**Several grinds**

Preheat the broiler. Cut the eggplants in half lengthwise and lightly coat the cut surfaces with the olive oil. Place the eggplants cut side up 4 inches under the broiler for 10 minutes. Remove and set aside to cool for a few minutes. Turn off the broiler and preheat the oven to 375 degrees F.

When cool enough to handle, use a sharp knife to cut out the eggplant pulp, leaving a ½-inch shell. Finely chop the pulp and combine it in a large bowl with ¼ cup of the Parmesan and all remaining ingredients. Mound the filling into the eggplant shells and sprinkle evenly with the remaining 2 tablespoons of Parmesan. Bake 25–30 minutes, until eggplant shells are fork-tender in their thickest part and Parmesan is browned. Serve hot.

Each serving provides:

260	Calories	32 g	Carbohydrate
13 g	Protein	791 mg	Sodium
10 g	Fat	21 mg	Cholesterol
3 g	Dietary Fiber		

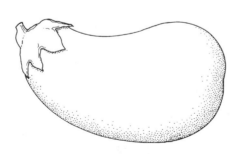

Pizza, Calzone, and Focaccia

Naples is the pizza capital of Italy, but pizza and other types of savory flat bread are enjoyed throughout the peninsula. In Italian cities, walk-up pizzerias appear on virtually every corner. Pizza is often sold by the slice from these stands and eaten piping hot with the hands. It is also enjoyed in *trattorias,* unpretentious dining establishments that serve traditional home cooking and are frequented by Italians of every age and social standing.

Pizza's popularity in Italy is almost matched by its popularity in the United States, where the pizza parlor is a common feature of the urban landscape. Styles of pizza vary on both sides of the Atlantic, from thin crusts topped with light tomato sauce to hearty, ingredient-laden deep-dish pies. The number of possible flavor combinations is nearly infinite, so we never tire of inventing new favorites. A substantial antipasto or vegetable salad can accompany side-dish pizzas to round out the meal. Main-course pizzas are satisfying with the addition of a leafy salad. And always, wine is an appropriate beverage with pizza.

The calzone, a savory stuffed turnover made with pizza dough, is eaten with a knife and fork. Bursting with tasty ingredients, it is well suited to large appetites. You may serve a single large calzone to be portioned at the table, or create individual ones. It is also fun to make miniature calzoni to be served as a charming and delicious antipasto.

Another Italian bread, focaccia, has long been a favorite snack food in Italy. It is beginning to turn up with some frequency in American homes and cafés, where it typically accompanies a meal. We enjoy focaccia as an appetizer or packed in the picnic basket, along with a vegetable salad and a good bottle of wine.

Pizza, calzone, and focaccia are rustic breads. They have been made for centuries in the most humble kitchens of Italy. All you really need to produce them in your own kitchen is a large bowl, a wooden spoon, a flat work surface, a flat baking pan, and a hot oven. However, there are several fun kitchen toys that can add to the pleasure of making Italian flat breads. They are discussed in the following list.

Tips and Tools

- To make sure you achieve the proper baking temperature, invest in a standard, inexpensive oven thermometer. Preheat the oven at least 15 minutes before baking, and check the thermometer before inserting the bread to see if it matches the dial setting. Adjust accordingly, and allow a few more minutes for the oven's temperature to stabilize.

- Yeast is activated only in water that is 105–115 degrees F. If you are inexperienced at manually judging the temperature of lukewarm water, you may wish to buy an instant-read thermometer to be certain your water is the proper temperature before adding the yeast.

- If the bowl you intend to use for activating the yeast is cold to the touch, rinse it with warm water or set it in the sun for a few minutes to take the chill off.

- Any large, clean, smooth, level counter or tabletop is suitable as a work surface for dough, although some bakers have a strong preference for wood.

- A pastry scraper is a heavy, flat piece of metal set into a handle, usually of wood. It is used to periodically scrape the work surface clean while you are preparing the dough, as well to cut the dough and to fold flour into the dough. A large spatula can serve the purpose, if need be.

- Pizza can be prepared and baked on a standard baking sheet, a round pizza pan, or a baking stone set directly in the oven. If purchasing a pan, select one of heavy-gauge stainless steel so it will heat uniformly and not warp.

- Baking stones are flat, unglazed clay tiles used to reproduce the effects of the traditional brick ovens used by Italian bakers. Lining an oven or grill, these tiles create an even distribution of heat for baking pizza, focaccia, and other breads. They can be purchased at cookware shops. Unglazed quarry tiles, available from home-building suppliers, are a good substitute. Place the tiles directly on top of the rack in the oven or on the grill.

- The baker's peel—a large, flat wooden paddle with a beveled edge—is used to transfer pizza, focaccia, or other bread to and from the baking stone. It is dusted with cornmeal to provide a smooth, nonstick medium for the dough. To transfer the pizza from the peel onto the baking stone, thrust the peel forward and pull it back sharply to dislodge the pizza and slide it off. If you are using a baking stone but do not own a peel, a baking sheet without a lip, dusted with cornmeal, can serve the same purpose.

Basic Pizza and Calzone Dough

VEGAN

Use bread flour or unbleached white flour. The flour measure is given as a range because the exact amount will vary depending on the day's humidity and other weather conditions. The temperature of the water used to start the yeast is important—if it is too hot, it will kill the yeast; if it is too cold, the yeast will not be activated.

Yield: 2 12-inch pizza crusts or 4 individual calzoni

Active dry yeast	¼	**ounce (1 envelope)**
Lukewarm water (105–115 degrees F.)	1½	**cups**
Olive oil	2	**tablespoons plus ½ teaspoon**
Salt	½	**teaspoon**
Unbleached flour	3½–4	**cups**

Place the yeast in a large bowl and add the warm water. Stir with a wooden spoon to dissolve the yeast, then set aside in a warm place until creamy in appearance, about 15 minutes. Stir in 2 tablespoons of oil and the salt, then add 2 cups of the flour. Stir to incorporate, using a large wooden spoon. The mixture will be very sticky at this point. Add 1 more cup of the flour and continue to stir until the dough begins to form a ball. Turn out onto a lightly floured work surface and knead the dough until it is soft and smooth, about 10 minutes, adding the remaining flour as needed, a bit at a time, until the dough is no longer sticky. Too much flour will result in a dry dough that can become a slightly tough crust, so don't add any more flour than necessary.

Lightly oil a large bowl with ½ teaspoon of oil. Place the dough ball in the oiled bowl, turn it to coat the entire surface with oil, and cover the bowl with a clean dish towel. Place the bowl in a warm, draft-free place for the dough to rise until doubled in volume, about 1½ hours. (An unlit oven or warm cupboard works well.) After it has risen, punch the dough down with your fist or fingertips to press out most of the air.

For pizza: Place the dough on a lightly floured work surface and divide it into 2 balls of equal size. Working with 1 ball at a time, flatten it with your hands into a circle about 4 inches in diameter and 1 inch thick. Now begin working from the center, pressing the dough outward with the heels of your hands. If the dough sticks to your hands, sprinkle lightly with flour. Push the dough into a 12-inch round that is slightly thicker at the edges. (You can also use a rolling pin to spread the dough into a 12-inch round.) If you are making only 1 pizza, the remaining dough ball may be wrapped tightly in plastic and frozen for up to 3 months. Thaw the dough at room temperature for a few hours before rolling out as directed. Proceed with the instructions of individual recipes.

For calzone: Place the dough on a lightly floured work surface and divide it into 4 balls of equal size. Working with 1 ball at a time, flatten it with your hands into a circle about 3 inches in diameter and 1 inch thick. Now begin working from the center, pressing the dough outward with the heels of your hands. If the dough sticks to your hands, sprinkle lightly with flour. Push the dough into an 8-inch round of even thickness. (Or use a rolling pin to spread the dough into an 8-inch round.) Shape the other 3 balls the same way. Proceed with the instructions of individual recipes.

Each pizza crust provides:

994	Calories	168 g	Carbohydrate
24 g	Protein	591 mg	Sodium
23 g	Fat	0 mg	Cholesterol
6 g	Dietary Fiber		

Each calzone crust provides:

497	Calories	84 g	Carbohydrate
12 g	Protein	295 mg	Sodium
11 g	Fat	0 mg	Cholesterol
3 g	Dietary Fiber		

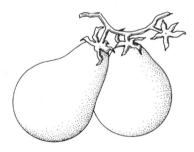

Pizza with Basil Pesto and Grilled Eggplant

ALMOST INSTANT

Basil Pesto, either store-bought or homemade, enlivens the tomato sauce to create a rich base for this pizza. Grilling the eggplant gives it a delightful smoky flavor. This is one of our favorite summertime pizzas.

Yield: 6 main-course servings

Pizza crust	1	12-inch crust
Yellow cornmeal	2	tablespoons
Eggplant	1	medium (1 pound)
Olive oil	2	tablespoons
Tomato sauce	4	tablespoons
Basil Pesto (see page 134)	3	tablespoons
Part-skim mozzarella cheese, shredded	6	ounces (1½ cups)
Fresh pear tomatoes	2	medium (¼ pound)

Prepare a pizza crust according to the directions on page 277 (or use a commercially prepared one). Place the uncooked pizza crust on a round pizza pan or baker's peel that has been sprinkled with the cornmeal. Preheat a coal or gas grill to high, about 500 degrees F., or preheat the broiler.

Remove and discard the stem end of the eggplant and cut the eggplant lengthwise into ½-inch-thick slices. Using half of the oil, brush one side of the eggplant slices and place them oiled side down on the grill, or oiled side up under the broiler. Cook for about 5 minutes, until slightly charred. Brush the other side of the slices with the remaining tablespoon of oil, turn, and continue to cook for 5 minutes, until eggplant is charred and soft. Set aside. Keep the grill hot, or if you are going to cook the pizza in the oven, preheat it to 450 degrees F.

Mix the tomato sauce and pesto together, then top the pizza crust with this mixture, leaving a 1-inch border free of sauce. Top the sauce with half of the cheese. Arrange the eggplant slices, fanning them out from the center, and top them with the remaining cheese. Thinly slice the tomatoes and arrange them evenly on top.

Transfer the pizza to the hot grill and cover the grill, or place the pizza in the hot oven. Bake for about 15 minutes, until the crust is crisp and the cheese has melted. Serve very hot.

Each serving provides:

365	Calories	39 g	Carbohydrate
13 g	Protein	322 mg	Sodium
17 g	Fat	17 mg	Cholesterol
2 g	Dietary Fiber		

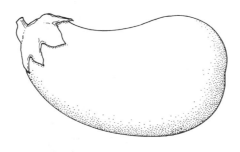

Pizza with Artichokes, Goat Cheese, Olives, and Oregano

ALMOST INSTANT

Ingredients common to Greek and Sicilian cuisines inspired this delicious pizza. Serve it with a big salad and red wine for a light supper.

Yield: 6 main-course servings

Pizza crust	1	12-inch crust
Yellow cornmeal	2	tablespoons
Fresh pear tomatoes	½	pound (3 medium)
Garlic	3	cloves, minced
Parmesan cheese, finely grated	2	tablespoons
Marinated artichoke hearts	1	6-ounce jar, drained
Greek feta cheese, crumbled	4	ounces (1 cup)
Kalamata olives, chopped	¼	cup
Fresh oregano, minced	1	tablespoon

Prepare a pizza crust according to the directions on page 277, or use a commercially prepared one. Place the uncooked crust on a round pizza pan or a baker's peel that has been sprinkled with the cornmeal. Preheat a coal or gas grill to high, about 500 degrees F., or preheat the oven to 450 degrees F.

Without peeling them, cut the tomatoes into quarters and put them in a blender. Add the garlic, puree until smooth, and set aside. Sprinkle the Parmesan cheese over the crust, then evenly top with the pureed tomatoes, leaving a 1-inch border free of sauce. Drain the artichoke hearts (you may want to reserve their marinade for salad dressing). Cut them into thin slices and distribute them evenly over the sauce. Top evenly with the feta, olives, and oregano.

Transfer the pizza to the hot grill and cover the grill, or place the pizza in the hot oven. Bake for about 15 minutes, until the crust is crisp and the cheese has softened and browned. Serve very hot.

Each serving provides:

306	Calories	39 g	Carbohydrate
9 g	Protein	588 mg	Sodium
13 g	Fat	18 mg	Cholesterol
2 g	Dietary Fiber		

Pizza Napoletana with Capers

ALMOST INSTANT

*The ultimate pizza in Naples, the motherland of pizza, is one topped
with only a fresh tomato sauce. This recipe includes capers, another
favorite ingredient of the region.*

Yield: 6 side-dish servings

Pizza crust	1	12-inch crust
Yellow cornmeal	2	tablespoons
Fresh pear tomatoes	½	pound (3 medium)
Fresh basil leaves, minced	1	tablespoon
Salt	¼	teaspoon
Extra virgin olive oil	1	teaspoon
Garlic	1	clove, minced
Parmesan cheese, finely grated	2	tablespoons
Capers, drained	1	tablespoon

Trim off and discard the stem ends of the tomatoes, but do not
peel. Puree them in a food processor. Add the basil, salt, olive
oil, and garlic. Pulse to combine. Allow to sit for up to 2 hours
while you prepare the crust.

Make a pizza crust according to the directions on page 277,
or use a commercially prepared one. Place the uncooked crust
on a round pizza pan or a baker's peel that has been sprinkled
with the cornmeal. Heat a coal or gas grill to high, about 500
degrees F., or preheat the oven to 450 degrees F.

Spread the tomato sauce over the crust, leaving a 1-inch border free of sauce, then top the sauce evenly with the Parmesan cheese. Distribute the capers across the top.

Transfer the pizza to the hot grill and cover the grill, or place in the hot oven. Bake for 10–12 minutes, until the crust is golden. Serve very hot.

Each serving provides:

209	Calories	34 g	Carbohydrate
5 g	Protein	243 mg	Sodium
5 g	Fat	1 mg	Cholesterol
2 g	Dietary Fiber		

Pizza with Three Cheeses and Dried Tomatoes

ALMOST INSTANT

This cheese pizza is a delightful combination of flavors. Choose it as a first course, or serve it with the Fennel and Radicchio Salad with Balsamic Vinaigrette (page 76) and Chianti for a light supper.

Yield: 8 side-dish servings

Pizza crust	1	**12-inch crust**
Yellow cornmeal	2	**tablespoons**
Dried tomatoes, minced	2	**tablespoons**
Extra virgin olive oil	1	**tablespoon**
Fontina cheese, grated	4	**ounces (1 cup)**
Asiago cheese, finely grated	¼	**cup**
Parmesan, finely grated	¼	**cup**

Prepare a pizza crust according to the directions on page 277, or use a commercially prepared one. Place the uncooked crust on a round pizza pan or a baker's peel that has been sprinkled with the cornmeal.

Meanwhile, reconstitute the tomatoes according to the directions on page 29. Drain well, chop, and set aside.

Preheat a coal or gas grill to high, about 500 degrees F., or preheat the oven to 450 degrees F.

Spread the oil over the crust, leaving a 1-inch border free of oil, then evenly distribute the fontina cheese over the oil. Distribute the reconstituted tomatoes, then top with the Asiago and Parmesan cheeses.

Transfer the pizza to the hot grill and cover the grill, or place in the hot oven. Bake for 10–12 minutes, until the crust is golden. Serve very hot.

Each serving provides:

235	Calories	25 g	Carbohydrate
9 g	Protein	291 mg	Sodium
11 g	Fat	22 mg	Cholesterol
1 g	Dietary Fiber		

Pizza with Salsa Verde, Roasted Peppers, and Goat Cheese

ALMOST INSTANT

Goat cheeses are not traditional ingredients of Italian cooking, but innovative cooks do occasionally use both firm, feta-style and soft goat cheeses. Here we call for soft chèvre because Italian goat cheese is rarely available in America. Take it from the refrigerator just before adding it to the pizza, as it is easier to handle when cold.

Yield: 4 main-course servings

Pizza crust	1	**12-inch crust**
Yellow cornmeal	2	**tablespoons**
Red bell pepper	1	**medium**
Piquant Green Sauce (see page 128)	½	**cup**
Red onion, thinly sliced	½	**cup**
Soft chèvre	2	**ounces**
Parmesan cheese, freshly grated	2	**tablespoons**

Prepare a pizza crust according to the directions on page 277, or use a commercially prepared one. Place the uncooked crust on a round pizza pan or a baker's peel that has been sprinkled with the cornmeal. Roast, peel, and seed the red pepper (see page 29) and cut into thin 1-inch-long strips. Set aside. Preheat a coal or gas grill to high, about 500 degrees F., or preheat the oven to 450 degrees F.

Spread the crust with the Piquant Green Sauce, leaving a 1-inch border free of sauce. Arrange the pepper strips evenly over the sauce. Scatter the onion slices evenly over the peppers. Use your hands to break the chèvre into small bits and distribute these across the pizza. Dust with the Parmesan.

Transfer the pizza to the hot grill and cover the grill, or place in the hot oven. Bake for 10–12 minutes, until the crust is golden. Serve very hot.

Each serving provides:

372	Calories	53 g	Carbohydrate
11 g	Protein	290 mg	Sodium
13 g	Fat	9 mg	Cholesterol
3 g	Dietary Fiber		

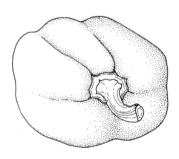

Pizza with Field Mushrooms, Fresh Herbs, and Gruyère Cheese

ALMOST INSTANT

Northern Italy shares a border with Switzerland, so Swiss-type cheeses sometimes appear in Northern Italian cuisine. This scrumptious pizza combines the earthy flavors of woodland mushrooms and herbs with the subtle sweetness of Gruyère. The herb mixture can include thyme, rosemary, oregano, marjoram, and any others you like. The paprika is a nontraditional touch that adds color and zest. Any combination of mushrooms can be used here. Try morels, chanterelles, and porcini mixed half and half with common button mushrooms. Certain types of field mushrooms release a great deal of liquid during cooking, so the sautéing time may vary.

Yield: 6 main-course servings

Pizza crust	1	12-inch crust
Yellow cornmeal	2	tablespoons
Fresh mushrooms, mixed	¾	pound
Unsalted butter	2	tablespoons
Garlic	3	cloves, minced
Salt		A pinch
Pepper		Several grinds
Fresh herbs, minced	2	teaspoons
Gruyère cheese, grated	¾	cup
Parmesan cheese, freshly grated	2	tablespoons
Ground paprika	¼	teaspoon

Prepare a pizza crust according to the directions on page 000, or use a commercially prepared one. Place the uncooked crust on a round pizza pan or a baker's peel that has been sprinkled with the cornmeal. Preheat a coal or gas grill to high, about 500 degrees F., or preheat the oven to 450 degrees F.

Carefully wash and dry the mushrooms, then chop or slice into small pieces. Melt the butter in a skillet over medium-high heat. Add the mushrooms and sauté, stirring frequently, for 5 minutes. Add the garlic, salt, and pepper. Sauté, stirring frequently, until the mushrooms have released their liquid and most of it has evaporated. Stir in the herbs.

Distribute the mushrooms over the crust, leaving a 1-inch border free of mushrooms. Evenly distribute the cheeses over the mushrooms, then dust with the paprika.

Transfer the pizza to the hot grill and cover the grill, or place in the hot oven. Bake for 10–12 minutes, until the crust is golden. Serve very hot.

Each serving provides:

313	Calories	38 g	Carbohydrate
11 g	Protein	203 mg	Sodium
13 g	Fat	28 mg	Cholesterol
2 g	Dietary Fiber		

Spicy Pizza with Baked Garlic, Fresh Tomatoes, and Fontina

ALMOST INSTANT

Roasted garlic pulp is the paste formed when whole heads of garlic are baked for a long time. The individual cloves soften and become mellow and sweet in flavor. The garlic may be roasted 1–2 days ahead of time. You may omit the chili flakes from this pizza if you are not fond of spicy food.

Yield: 6 side-dish servings

Roasted garlic bulb	1	**large**
Pizza crust	1	**12-inch crust**
Yellow cornmeal	2	**tablespoons**
Dried red chili flakes	¼	**teaspoon**
Fresh pear tomatoes	½	**pound (about 3 medium)**
Fontina cheese, grated	1½	**ounces**

Bake 1 large bulb of garlic according to the directions on page 30. Set aside to cool.

Prepare a pizza crust according to the directions on page 277, or use a commercially prepared one. Place the uncooked crust on a round pizza pan or a baker's peel that has been sprinkled with the cornmeal. Preheat a coal or gas grill to high, about 500 degrees F., or preheat the oven to 450 degrees F.

When the baked bulb is cool enough to handle, squeeze out the soft garlic paste and spread it evenly over the crust, leaving a 1-inch border free of garlic. Distribute the chili flakes over the garlic. Slice the tomatoes crosswise into thin circles and arrange evenly on the pizza. Top evenly with the fontina.

Transfer to the hot grill and cover the grill, or place in the hot oven. Bake for 10–12 minutes, until the crust is golden. Serve very hot.

Each serving provides:

230	Calories	37 g	Carbohydrate
7 g	Protein	158 mg	Sodium
6 g	Fat	8 mg	Cholesterol
2 g	Dietary Fiber		

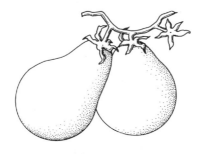

Calzone with Onions, Olives, and Gorgonzola

This calzone combines sautéed sweet onions with bitter olives and Gorgonzola cheese for an exquisite explosion of aroma and flavor. The recipe makes 4 hefty calzoni, which can be served individually for big appetites or divided in half for light eaters. If you have a grill, the calzoni could be the centerpiece of a casual outdoor dinner party. Begin the meal with a showy antipasto such as the Fresh Mozzarella with Tomatoes and Basil (page 68), and accompany the main course with a tart, leafy salad and a barely chilled California Pinot Noir.

Yield: 8 main-course servings

Basic calzone dough	1	**recipe**
Red onions	1¼	**pounds (2 large)**
Olive oil	2	**tablespoons**
Dry oil-cured black olives, pitted and chopped	¼	**cup**
Gorgonzola cheese, crumbled	3	**ounces (⅔ cup)**
Yellow cornmeal	¼	**cup**

Make the calzone dough according to the directions on page 277.

While it is rising, cut the onions in half lengthwise, then thinly slice each half. Heat 2 tablespoons of olive oil in a large skillet over medium heat. Add the onions to the skillet and toss quickly with tongs to distribute the oil. Sauté, stirring often, until the onions have softened and most of their liquid has evaporated, about 20 minutes. It is fine for the onions to brown a little, but reduce the heat if they seem to be browning too quickly. Preheat the oven to 425 degrees F.

Roll out the calzone dough as directed on page 278. Top half of each dough circle with one quarter of the onions, leaving a 1-inch border, then top the onions with one quarter of the olives and cheese. Fold the dough over and press, enclosing the filling in a turnover-shaped packet. Crimp the edges with a fork to seal them firmly. Place the calzoni on a baking sheet or a baker's peel dusted with the cornmeal. Bake for 30–35 minutes, until golden brown. Allow to cool slightly before serving.

Each serving provides:

388	Calories	55 g	Carbohydrate
10 g	Protein	462 mg	Sodium
14 g	Fat	10 mg	Cholesterol
3 g	Dietary Fiber		

Calzone with Escarole, Ricotta, Raisins, and Pine Nuts

These flavors do not combine to be too sweet, as you might suspect from the raisins. The calzoni are perfectly wonderful sliced and served as an antipasto or served whole as a main course. Escarole is a bitter green favored by Italian cooks. Chard or spinach could be substituted for it.

Yield: 8 main-course servings

Basic calzone dough	1	**recipe**
Pine nuts	2	**tablespoons**
Escarole	½	**pound**
Olive oil	1	**tablespoon**
Yellow onion	1	**medium, diced**
Golden raisins	2	**tablespoons, minced**
Garlic	3	**cloves**
Part-skim ricotta cheese	1	**cup**
Egg	1	**medium**
Salt	½	**teaspoon**
Pepper		**Several grinds**
Yellow cornmeal	¼	**cup**

Make the calzone dough according to the directions on page 277.

While it is rising, toast the pine nuts (see page 31) and set them aside. Separate the leaves of the escarole from the core and wash them carefully. Place the wet leaves in a large pan, cover, and cook over medium heat 10 minutes, until wilted. Drain, pressing out as much water as possible. Chop the escarole coarsely.

Heat the olive oil in a sauté pan over medium heat and sauté the onion 5 minutes. Stir in the raisins and garlic, then the escarole, and cook another 1–2 minutes. Transfer to a bowl and combine with the ricotta, egg, pine nuts, salt, and pepper. Preheat the oven to 425 degrees F.

Roll out the dough as directed on page 278. Top half of each dough circle with one quarter of the filling, leaving a 1-inch border. Fold the dough over, joining the edges, and press, enclosing the filling in a turnover-shaped packet. Crimp the edges with a fork to seal them firmly. Place the calzoni on a baking sheet or a baker's peel dusted with the cornmeal. Bake for 30–35 minutes, until golden brown. Allow to cool slightly before serving.

Each serving provides:

391	Calories	58 g	Carbohydrate
12 g	Protein	353 mg	Sodium
12 g	Fat	37 mg	Cholesterol
3 g	Dietary Fiber		

Focaccia with Fresh Rosemary and Sautéed Onions

This focaccia is rich with the earthy flavor of rosemary and the sweetness of sautéed red onions. It makes a terrific snack alone or a scrumptious addition to an antipasti table. Pack it with a chunky vegetable salad and a light red wine for a fine picnic feast.

Yield: 12 side-dish servings (24 3-inch squares)

The dough

Active dry yeast	¼	ounce (1 envelope)
Lukewarm water (105–115 degrees F.)	1½	cups
Olive oil	3	tablespoons plus ½ teaspoon
Salt	½	teaspoon
Unbleached flour	3½–4	cups
Fresh rosemary leaves, minced	¼	cup

The focaccia

Red onions	2	pounds, thinly sliced
Olive oil	¼	cup
Coarse sea salt	1½	teaspoons
Fresh rosemary sprigs, 1 inch in length	½	cup

Place the yeast in a large bowl and add the warm water. Stir with a wooden spoon to dissolve the yeast, then set aside in a warm place until creamy in appearance, about 15 minutes. Stir in 2 tablespoons of oil and the salt, then add 2 cups of the flour and the minced rosemary. Stir to incorporate, using a large wooden spoon. The mixture will be very sticky at this point, Add 1 more cup of the flour and continue to stir until the dough begins to form a ball. Turn out onto a lightly floured work surface and knead the dough until it is soft and smooth, about 10 minutes, adding the remaining flour as needed, a bit at a time, until the dough is no longer sticky. Too much flour will result in a dry dough that can become a slightly tough crust, so don't add any more flour than necessary.

Rub a large bowl with ½ teaspoon of oil. Place the dough ball in the oiled bowl, turn it to coat the entire surface with oil, and cover the bowl with a clean dish towel. Place the bowl in a warm, draft-free place for the dough to rise until doubled in volume, about 1½ hours. (An unlit oven or warm cupboard works well.) After it has risen, punch the dough down with your fist or fingertips to press out most of the air.

Transfer the dough to a lightly floured work surface and slap it down firmly a few times. Place 1 tablespoon of olive oil in a lipped 12 × 18-inch baking sheet. Distribute the oil evenly over the bottom and sides of the sheet. Place the dough in the center, and, pressing with your hands from the middle of the dough, carefully stretch it until it covers the sheet completely in an even layer. Cover with a damp cloth and set aside to rise again for 45 minutes.

While the dough is rising for the second time, heat 2 tablespoons of the olive oil over medium heat. Add the onions and toss with tongs to distribute the oil. Sauté for 12–15 minutes, tossing occasionally, until onions are soft and almost all their liquid has evaporated.

Preheat the oven to 425 degrees F. When the dough has finished rising for the second time, use your fingertips to gently dimple the surface of the dough with shallow indentations. Coat the top with 2 tablespoons of olive oil and dust evenly with the salt. Distribute the onions evenly over the dough and bake 25 minutes. Remove from the oven and distribute the rosemary sprigs evenly over the bread. Bake 5–7 minutes longer, until the bottom of the bread is lightly browned (use a spatula to lift the bread gently and check for browning).

Cut into 3-inch squares and serve hot or at room temperature.

Each serving provides:

257	Calories	39 g	Carbohydrate
5 g	Protein	356 mg	Sodium
9 g	Fat	0 mg	Cholesterol
3 g	Dietary Fiber		

Focaccia with Garlic and Olives

VEGAN

How delicious can home-baked bread be? Experiment with different seasonings for focaccia and you will find out. This version may be one of the best.

Yield: 12 side-dish servings (24 3-inch squares)

The dough

Active dry yeast	¼	ounce (1 envelope)
Lukewarm water (105–115 degrees F.)	1½	cups
Olive oil	3	tablespoons plus ½ teaspoon
Salt	½	teaspoon
Unbleached flour	3½–4	cups
Garlic	6	cloves, minced

The focaccia

Water-packed green olives	1	cup
Olive oil	2	tablespoons
Coarse sea salt	1	teaspoon

Place the yeast in a large bowl and add the warm water. Stir with a wooden spoon to dissolve the yeast, then set aside in a warm place until creamy in appearance, about 15 minutes. Stir in 2 tablespoons of oil and the salt, then add 2 cups of the flour and the minced garlic. Stir to incorporate, using a large wooden spoon. The mixture will be very sticky at this point. Add 1 more cup of the flour and continue to stir until the dough begins to form a ball. Turn out onto a lightly floured work surface and knead the dough until it is soft and smooth, about 10 minutes, adding the remaining flour as needed, a bit at a time, until the dough is no longer sticky. Too much flour will result in a dry dough that can become a slightly tough crust, so don't add any more flour than necessary.

Rub a large bowl with ½ teaspoon of oil. Place the dough ball in the oiled bowl, turn it to coat the entire surface with oil, and cover the bowl with a clean dish towel. Place the bowl in a warm, draft-free place for the dough to rise until doubled in volume, about 1½ hours. (An unlit oven or warm cupboard works well.) After it has risen, punch the dough down with your fist or fingertips to press out most of the air.

Transfer the dough to a lightly floured work surface and slap it down firmly a few times. Place 1 tablespoon of olive oil in a lipped 12 × 18-inch baking sheet. Distribute the oil evenly over the bottom and sides of the sheet. Place the dough in the center, and, pressing with your hands from the middle of the dough, carefully stretch it until it covers the sheet completely in an even layer. Cover with a damp cloth and set aside to rise again for 45 minutes.

While the dough is rising for the second time, pit the olives and cut the olives approximately in half.

Preheat the oven to 425 degrees F. When the dough has finished rising for the second time, use your fingertips to gently dimple the surface of the dough with shallow indentations. Distribute the olive halves over the dough, cut side down, pressing to embed the olives in the dough. Coat the top of the dough evenly with olive oil and dust evenly with 2 tablespoons of the salt. Bake 30–35 minutes, until the bottom is lightly browned (use a spatula to lift the bread gently and check for browning).

Cut into 3-inch squares and serve hot or at room temperature.

Each serving provides:

215	Calories	32 g	Carbohydrate
5 g	Protein	532 mg	Sodium
7 g	Fat	0 mg	Cholesterol
﹨1 g	Dietary Fiber		

Roxanne's Focaccia

VEGAN

Roxanne O'Brien—friend, artist, and chef extraordinaire—serves up wonderful focaccia bread and other delicious treats at First Immigrant Cafe in Sacramento. Here she shares one of her favorite breads with us. Her technique differs a bit from ours, which demonstrates the flexibility involved in creating this rustic bread.

Yield: 12 side-dish servings (24 3-inch pieces)

Olive oil	7	tablespoons plus 1 teaspoon
Yellow onion	1	medium, diced
Red bell pepper	½	medium, diced
Garlic	6	cloves, minced
Fresh basil leaves, chopped	½	cup
Active dry yeast	¼	ounce (1 envelope)
Lukewarm water (105–115 degrees F.)	2	cups
Unbleached flour	5½	cups
Brown sugar	1	teaspoon
Salt	1	tablespoon
Yellow cornmeal	2	tablespoons

Heat 1 tablespoon of the olive oil in a pan at a medium setting and sauté the onion, bell pepper, and garlic for 10 minutes. Cool completely, then stir in the basil. Set aside.

In a small mixing bowl, dissolve the yeast in the lukewarm water. Set aside in a warm place until creamy in appearance, about 15 minutes. In a medium-size mixing bowl, combine 2 cups of the flour, the brown sugar, and the salt. Add the cooled onion mixture to the flour mixture and stir with a wooden spoon.

Stir in the yeast mixture, then add the remaining flour and ¼ cup olive oil. Mix the dough with your hands until it holds together in a ball, about 1 minute. Coat with 1 teaspoon of olive oil, cover the bowl with plastic wrap, and set in a warm place for about one and a half hours, or until doubled in volume.

Line a 12 × 18-inch baking sheet with parchment paper and sprinkle with the cornmeal. Punch down the dough and form into a smooth ball. Place this in the center of the baking sheet and flatten it out with your hands to completely cover the pan about 1 inch thick, dimpling the top of the dough with your fingertips. Coat the top lightly with 1 tablespoon of olive oil and allow to rise again for a half hour.

Meanwhile, preheat the oven to 375 degrees F. After the second rising, bake the focaccia for about 30 minutes, or until it feels light when lifted slightly from the pan. Brush the top with the remaining 1 tablespoon of olive oil. Cool on a rack. Cut into 3-inch squares.

Each serving provides:

295	Calories	47 g	Carbohydrate
6 g	Protein	583 mg	Sodium
9 g	Fat	0 mg	Cholesterol
2 g	Dietary Fiber		

Tortas and Frittate

Italian-style egg dishes are hearty, full-flavored, and satisfying enough to serve as a casual evening entrée at our tables, as they often do in Italy, where the traditional midday meal is hearty and has several courses, and lighter suppers are commonplace. Frittate and tortas are versatile, however, and we also enjoy them as antipasti or for brunch or lunch.

To build a satisfying meal around one of these dishes, begin with a substantial antipasti platter and include salad and bread. We also recommend packing one in your picnic basket for a sunset dinner on the beach or hillside, since these sturdy egg preparations travel well.

The Italian frittata is related to the French omelette in that both combine beaten eggs with savory ingredients and seasonings, but the similarities end there. The omelette is light and airy and always served hot, while the frittata is more dense and can be served at any temperature.

Torta is the Italian name for any pie, be it sweet or savory. Our savory tortas combine vegetables, eggs, and cheese in a flaky pastry crust. The result is rustic, robust, and delicious. If you are intimidated by the thought of preparing a piecrust from scratch, or if time is short, purchase a ready-to-bake one.

To Italians, egg dishes are not occasional indulgences. They are staples, enjoyed year-round, in endless variety. Master the simple preparation methods, and they will become regulars on your table as well.

Tips and Tools

- Those who are watching their cholesterol intake may prepare our frittata recipes with 4 whole eggs and 3 egg whites, in place of 6 whole eggs. This will reduce the cholesterol content by one-third.

- A well-seasoned 10-inch cast-iron skillet or another heavy-gauge oven-proof pan is essential for making frittate.

- Frittate are cooked on top of the stove until the bottom of the egg mixture is firm and golden brown and the top is not quite set. In Italy, frittate are typically flipped at this point to finish cooking. We prefer to avoid this awkward task by finishing our frittate in the oven or under the broiler.

- Tortas may be baked in glass or ceramic pie pans or quiche dishes. A fluted tart pan with removable sides makes a particularly pretty presentation.

- A pastry cutter facilitates the blending of butter and flour for pastry dough and is much faster than the alternative, which is to use two knives to cut in the butter.

- A marble or heavy wood rolling pin is essential for rolling out the pastry dough for tortas.
- Baking weights are used to prevent the bottom of a pastry crust from ballooning when it is partially baked before filling. You can buy them at a cookware store. As an economical alternative, we keep a supply of dried beans in our pantries, specifically labeled for this purpose.

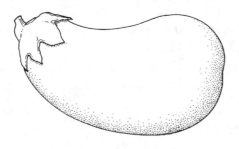

Pastry Crust

This versatile pastry crust can be used for either savory or sweet pies. A few tries will convince you that there is nothing difficult about making piecrust.

Yield: 2 9- or 10-inch pastry crusts

Unbleached flour	1	**cup**
Whole wheat pastry flour	½	**cup**
Salt	½	**teaspoon**
Unsalted butter (cold)	½	**cup (1 stick)**
Ice water	¼	**cup**

Sift flours and salt together into a bowl. Slice butter into about 8 pieces and add to the flour. Use a pastry cutter or 2 knives to cut the butter into the flour mixture until the mixture resembles coarse crumbs. Add water, 1 tablespoon at a time, stirring to incorporate after each addition. After the last addition, mixture will hold together in a ball. Divide into 2 portions, wrap separately in wax paper, and set aside in the refrigerator for 1 hour. (If you won't need 2 crusts, you may freeze 1 portion of dough for later use. Defrost frozen dough in the refrigerator for several hours before rolling out.) Remove the dough from the refrigerator and allow to sit at room temperature for 15 minutes before rolling out.

Roll out each portion on a floured board into a circle large enough to line a 9- or 10-inch glass or ceramic pie or quiche pan. Place the dough in the pan, making sure it sits flush against the sides and bottom. Trim off any overhanging dough. Use your fingers to crimp the edge of the dough into a decorative pattern. Cover the pan with a damp tea towel to prevent the crust from drying out while you make the filling.

This crust may also be made in a food processor, following the manufacturer's directions.

Each crust provides:

308	Calories	28 g	Carbohydrate
12 g	Protein	612 mg	Sodium
17 g	Fat	134 mg	Cholesterol
6 g	Dietary Fiber		

Artichoke Olive Torta with Oregano and Parmesan

The flavors of oil-cured olives, oregano, and garlic define this dish as a Southern Italian classic. The texture and taste of freshly cooked artichokes is vastly superior to those of canned varieties. Therefore, we recommend preparing this dish at the peak of artichoke season, when prices and quality are at their best. Once you have tried the artichoke-trimming technique described in the instructions, you will realize how simple it is, and the results will seem worth the moderate investment of time.

Yield: 8 main-course servings

Pastry Crust	1	9- or 10-inch crust
Fresh artichokes	5	medium (about 2 pounds)
Olive oil	1	tablespoon
Dried red chili flakes	¼	teaspoon
White onion	1	large, diced
Garlic	3	cloves, minced
Dried oregano	1	teaspoon
Salt	¼	teaspoon
Dry white wine	⅓	cup
Dry oil-cured black olives, pitted and chopped	⅓	cup
Fresh Italian parsley, minced	2	tablespoons
Eggs	3	large
Parmesan cheese, finely grated	½	cup
Freshly grated nutmeg	¼	teaspoon

Preheat the oven to 375 degrees F. Prepare the pastry crust according to the directions on page 309. (Alternately, you may use a commercially prepared ready-to-bake crust.) Line a tart or pie pan with the crust and crimp the edge.

Pierce the bottom of the crust with a fork in several places. Lay a sheet of foil inside the crust and conform its shape to that of the dish. The foil should cover the crimped edge of the crust. Place about 1 cup of dried beans (or commercial baking weights) over the foil to prevent the bottom of the crust from ballooning. Bake for 10 minutes. Remove the beans, saving them for your next pastry crust. Remove the foil and set the crust aside.

Prepare acidulated water in a large bowl by combining 2 quarts of cold water with 6 tablespoons of lemon juice or vinegar. Set aside near your work surface.

Trim the artichokes, working with 1 artichoke at a time. Use your hands to snap off all the outer leaves until you get down to the pale leaves at the center. Use a sharp knife to cut off the leaf tips, leaving only the base and yellowish green leaves. Cut off ¼ inch of the stem end, then peel the stem and the bottom of each artichoke. Proceed until you have trimmed all the artichokes in this manner, dropping each artichoke into the acidulated water as you finish. Next, remove the artichoke hearts from the water 1 at a time and quarter them from stem to top. Use a paring knife or melon baller to scrape out the fuzzy "choke" portion. Finally, slice each quarter lengthwise into thirds or fourths, depending on their size. You want wedges about ¼-inch thick. As you go, drop the artichoke pieces back into the acidulated water.

Heat the olive oil in a skillet or sauté pan at medium-high and add the chili flakes and onion. Stir and sauté about 3 minutes, then add the garlic, artichokes, oregano, and salt. Sauté 7 minutes, stirring frequently. Add the wine and immediately cover the pan. Reduce heat to medium-low and cook 5 minutes. Very little liquid should remain in the pan. If the mixture is watery, cook for a few more minutes over medium heat, stirring frequently, to evaporate the liquid. Stir in the olives and parsley, and pour half of the mixture evenly into the pastry crust.

Meanwhile, in a small bowl, lightly beat the eggs with the Parmesan and nutmeg. Pour half the eggs over the artichoke mixture in the crust, then add remaining artichoke mixture, and top with remaining egg. Gently shake the dish to settle the ingredients and bake for 25–30 minutes, until the egg is set and the top is nicely browned. Allow to cool for 30 minutes, then cut into wedges and serve warm or at room temperature.

Each serving provides:

231	Calories	21 g	Carbohydrate
9 g	Protein	459 mg	Sodium
13 g	Fat	100 mg	Cholesterol
5 g	Dietary Fiber		

Asparagus and Leek Torta

This is one of those dishes that we crave, and once spring arrives we satisfy our longing by eating it often. Serve with a salad, focaccia, and cheese as a light supper or Sunday brunch.

Yield: 6 main-course servings

Pastry Crust	1	**9- or 10-inch crust**
Asparagus	1	**pound**
Leeks	½	**pound**
Olive oil	1	**tablespoon**
Salt	¼	**teaspoon**
Pepper		**Several grinds**
Eggs	2	**large**
Lowfat milk	½	**cup**
Gruyère cheese, grated	4	**ounces (1½ cups)**
Freshly grated nutmeg	½	**teaspoon**

Preheat the oven to 375 degrees F. Prepare a pastry crust according to the directions on page 309, using a 9-inch, high-walled pie or quiche pan. (You may substitute a commercially prepared ready-to-bake crust, if you wish.) Line the pan with the crust and crimp the edge.

Pierce the bottom of the crust with a fork in several places. Lay a sheet of foil inside the crust and conform its shape to that of the dish. The foil should cover the crimped edge of the crust. Place about 1 cup of dried beans (or commercial baking weights) in the dish to prevent the bottom of the crust from ballooning. Bake for 10 minutes. Remove the beans, saving them for your next pastry crust. Remove the foil and set the crust aside. Reduce the oven temperature to 350 degrees F.

Meanwhile, cut off and discard the tough green ends of the leeks. Slice the white portion in half lengthwise and rinse under cold water to remove any dirt caught in the layers. Shake off as much water as possible, then slice into ¾-inch lengths. Toss with ½ tablespoon of the oil, ⅛ teaspoon salt, and a few grinds of pepper. Arrange the leeks on a baking dish in a single layer and bake 20 minutes until they just begin to get tender.

Meanwhile, carefully wash the asparagus to remove any dirt caught in the buds. Pat it dry. Snap off and discard the tough ends, then cut the spears diagonally into 1-inch-long pieces. Toss them with the remaining ½ tablespoon of oil, ⅛ teaspoon salt, and a few grinds of pepper. Arrange them in a baking dish in a single layer and bake 8 minutes, until they just begin to get tender. They will finish baking in the torta filling.

Crack the eggs into a medium-size bowl and lightly beat them with a whisk, then whisk in the milk, cheese, and nutmeg. Arrange the leeks evenly over the bottom of the crust, then top evenly with the asparagus. Pour the egg and cheese mixture over the top. Bake for 30–35 minutes, until the crust is golden and the filling is set. Cool for 10–15 minutes before serving.

Each serving provides:

209	Calories	13 g	Carbohydrate
9 g	Protein	209 mg	Sodium
14 g	Fat	85 mg	Cholesterol
1 g	Dietary Fiber		

Eggplant Torta with Ricotta Cheese and Mustard

The flavor of this pie is earthy and interesting. The egg mixture laced with ricotta and mustard binds the filling to complete this wonderful marriage of flavors.

Yield: 8 main-course servings

Eggplants	1½	**pounds (2 small)**
Salt	1	**teaspoon**
Pastry Crust	1	**9- or 10-inch crust**
Olive oil	2	**tablespoons**
Fresh Italian parsley, minced	¼	**cup**
Garlic	2	**cloves, minced**
Pepper		**Several grinds**
Eggs	3	**large**
Part-skim ricotta cheese	½	**cup**
Parmesan cheese, finely grated	2	**tablespoons**
Dijon mustard	1	**tablespoon**

Peel and dice the eggplants. Place the pieces in a colander and toss with the salt. Place the colander over a deep bowl and set aside to drain for 45 minutes to 1 hour. Rinse the eggplant briefly under cold water, then pat dry with a clean tea towel. Preheat the oven to 375 degrees F.

Meanwhile, prepare the pastry crust according to the directions on page 309. (You may substitute a commercially prepared ready-to-bake crust, if you prefer.) Line a 9- or 10-inch, high-walled quiche or pie pan with the crust and crimp the edge.

Pierce the bottom of the crust with a fork in several places. Lay a sheet of foil inside the crust and conform its shape to that of the dish. The foil should cover the crimped edge of the crust. Place about 1 cup of dried beans (or commercial baking weights) into the dish to prevent the bottom of the crust from ballooning. Bake for 10 minutes. Remove the beans, saving them for your next pastry crust. Remove the foil and set the crust aside.

Heat the olive oil over medium-high heat in a large skillet. Add the garlic and parsley, stir, then add the eggplant. Cook 5 minutes, stirring constantly. The eggplant will immediately soak up all the oil, but will begin to release its moisture within the allotted cooking time. Decrease the heat to medium and sauté, stirring occasionally, 10–12 more minutes, until the eggplant cubes are tender but not falling apart.

Meanwhile, place the eggs in a large bowl and beat lightly with a whisk. Add the ricotta, Parmesan, mustard, and pepper, and whisk to combine. When the eggplant is done, stir it into the egg mixture, then pour the combined mixture into the pastry crust. Shake the dish to settle the ingredients and bake 25–30 minutes, until the top is lightly browned and a knife inserted into the center of the torta comes out clean. Allow to cool for 10–15 minutes before slicing. Serve hot, warm, or at room temperature.

Each serving provides:

204	Calories	15 g	Carbohydrate
7 g	Protein	251 mg	Sodium
13 g	Fat	102 mg	Cholesterol
1 g	Dietary Fiber		

Torta with Chard, Ricotta, and Sage

The flavors in this torta are a classic Italian combination—chard, ricotta, and nutmeg. Sage provides an earthy note.

Yield: 8 main-course servings

Pastry Crust	1	9- or 10-inch crust
Swiss chard	1½	pounds
Olive oil	1	tablespoon
Dry sherry	1	tablespoon
Yellow onion	1	medium, diced
Dried sage	1	teaspoon
Eggs	2	large
Part-skim ricotta cheese	1	cup
Freshly grated nutmeg	¼	teaspoon
Salt	¼	teaspoon

Preheat the oven to 375 degrees F. Prepare a pastry crust according to the directions on page 309, using a 9-inch, high-walled pie or quiche pan. (You may substitute a commercially prepared ready-to-bake crust, if you wish.) Line the pan with the crust and crimp the edge.

Pierce the bottom of the crust with a fork in several places. Lay a sheet of foil inside the crust and conform its shape to that of the dish. The foil should cover the crimped edge of the crust. Place 1 cup of dried beans (or commercial baking weights) in the dish to prevent the bottom of the crust from ballooning. Bake for 10 minutes. Remove the beans, saving them for your next pastry crust. Remove the foil and set the crust aside.

Meanwhile, wash the chard but do not dry it, and coarsely chop. Place the wet chard in a large pan that has a tight-fitting lid, cover, and cook over medium heat until it wilts, about 5 minutes. Drain thoroughly in a colander, gently pressing it with the back of a wooden spoon to remove as much water as possible.

Heat the olive oil and sherry in a skillet over medium heat, then add the onion and sage. Sauté for several minutes, until the onion is translucent. Crack the eggs into a medium bowl and lightly beat them. Stir in the ricotta cheese, nutmeg, and salt. Fold in the chard and onion mixture, and stir to combine. Pour into the prepared crust and bake for 30–35 minutes, until the crust is golden and the filling is set. Cool for about 10 minutes before serving.

Each serving provides:

194	Calories	15 g	Carbohydrate
8 g	Protein	365 mg	Sodium
12 g	Fat	78 mg	Cholesterol
1 g	Dietary Fiber		

Zucchini Frittata with Mint

The ingredients used in this fragrant frittata are readily available in any grocery store, though you can also grow them easily in the backyard garden.

Yield: 6 side-dish servings

Dried tomatoes, minced	2	**tablespoons**
Eggs	6	**large**
Fresh mint, minced	½	**cup**
Fresh Italian parsley, minced	¼	**cup**
Salt	¼	**teaspoon**
Pepper		**Several grinds**
Zucchini	1	**pound (3 medium)**
Olive oil	1	**tablespoon**
Yellow onion, minced	½	**cup**
Dried red chili flakes	¼	**teaspoon, crushed**

If they are too hard to mince, reconstitute the dried tomatoes by soaking them for 15–30 minutes in hot water. Preheat the oven to 400 degrees F.

Crack the eggs into a large bowl and lightly beat them with a whisk. Stir in the mint, parsley, salt, and pepper. Set aside. Trim the ends from the zucchini and slice into ¼-inch-thick rounds. Heat the oil in a 10-inch cast-iron skillet over medium heat and add the onion, zucchini, and chili flakes. Sauté, stirring occasionally, until the zucchini begin to turn golden brown, about 15 minutes. The onion will caramelize and take on a medium brown color. Stir frequently during the last 5 minutes of cooking so that the onion does not burn. Add the minced tomatoes to the eggs and pour this mixture over the zucchini, stirring to evenly distribute. Reduce the heat to low and cook, uncovered, for about 10 minutes until all but the top is set. Place the skillet in the oven and cook until the top is set, 6–8 minutes.

Allow the frittata to cool a few minutes, then invert it onto a plate or serve it from the pan. Cut into wedges and serve hot or at room temperature.

Each serving provides:

116	Calories	5 g	Carbohydrate
8 g	Protein	176 mg	Sodium
7 g	Fat	213 mg	Cholesterol
1 g	Dietary Fiber		

Sweet Red Pepper Frittata with Capers and Fresh Basil

A blending of summery flavors and colors makes this dish an excellent entrée for a warm-weather brunch or light supper. Piquant Green Sauce (page 128) would be a wonderful topping if you have some on hand, though the frittata is quite delightful simply as it is. If you are making a supper of it, include a tart salad or antipasto dish such as the Marinated Garbanzo Beans with Onions, Pepperoncini, and Fontina (page 48) and a crusty Italian bread.

Yield: 6 main-course servings

Red bell pepper	**1**	**small**
Eggs	**6**	**large**
Parmesan cheese, finely grated	**¼**	**cup**
Capers, drained and minced	**2**	**tablespoons**
Pepper		**Several grinds**
Olive oil	**1½**	**tablespoons**
Garlic	**2**	**cloves, minced**
Fresh basil leaves	**½**	**cup, slivered**

Remove and discard the stem, seeds, and white membranes of the pepper. Slice the pepper into thin 1-inch-long strips and set aside. In a bowl, lightly beat the eggs with the Parmesan, capers, and pepper. Set aside.

Place the oil in a well-seasoned cast-iron skillet and use a rubber spatula or brush to make sure the bottom and sides of the pan are entirely coated with oil. Heat the oil over medium heat, add the garlic, and cook 1 minute. Add the pepper strips, and stir and sauté about 7 minutes, until the pepper has released its liquid and most of it has evaporated. Stir in the basil, then distribute the mixture evenly over the bottom of the pan.

Preheat the broiler. Pour the egg mixture evenly over the pepper mixture and reduce heat to low. Cook, stirring occasionally, until frittata is firm on the bottom and only a thin layer of uncooked egg remains on the top. Place the skillet under the broiler and cook 1–2 minutes, until the top is firm and lightly browned.

Allow the frittata to cool a few minutes, then invert it onto a plate or serve it from the pan if it is sticking. Cut into wedges and serve hot, at room temperature, or even cold.

Each serving provides:

132	Calories	3 g	Carbohydrate
8 g	Protein	188 mg	Sodium
10 g	Fat	216 mg	Cholesterol
0 g	Dietary Fiber		

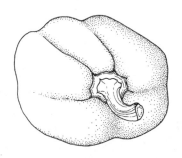

Frittata with Pasta, Peas, and Gorgonzola

Leftover cooked pasta is common in Italian kitchens, and we are sure that an inspired home cook decided to mix it with some eggs one day to create a new type of frittata. In this recipe, the peas are suspended in the mixture and the Gorgonzola cheese lends a pungent flavor. Serve this as a main dish with a mixed green salad and Grilled Italian Garlic Bread (page 40).

Yield: 6 main-course servings

Dried spaghetti	8	**ounces**
Eggs	6	**large**
Unsalted butter	1	**tablespoon**
Yellow onion, minced	½	**cup**
Dried oregano	1	**teaspoon**
Salt	¼	**teaspoon**
Pepper		**Several grinds**
Peas, fresh or frozen	1	**cup**
Gorgonzola cheese, crumbled	3	**ounces (½ cup)**

Bring several quarts of water to a boil for the pasta and cook it until al dente. Drain and set aside. (You may also use leftover cooked pasta—any ribbon or strand variety will work.)

Preheat the oven to 350 degrees F. Crack the eggs into a large bowl and lightly beat them with a whisk. Stir in the salt and pepper, and set aside. Melt the butter in a 10-inch cast-iron skillet over medium heat and add the onion and oregano. Sauté gently for about 5 minutes. Stir the onion mixture, peas, and cheese into the eggs until well distributed. Put the cooked pasta in the skillet and distribute it evenly over the bottom. Pour the egg mixture over the pasta, using a wooden spoon to distribute it among the pasta strands. Turn the heat to low and cook, uncovered, for about 10 minutes. Place the skillet in the oven to finish cooking the eggs and to melt the cheese, about 8 minutes.

Allow the frittata to cool a few minutes, then invert it onto a plate or serve it from the pan. Cut into wedges and serve hot or at room temperature.

Each serving provides:

307	Calories	33 g	Carbohydrate
16 g	Protein	433 mg	Sodium
12 g	Fat	231 mg	Cholesterol
2 g	Dietary Fiber		

Potato and Rosemary Frittata

*This is a wonderful Italian twist on the classic American breakfast—
eggs and potatoes. It comes together quickly and has a comforting
quality.*

Yield: 6 main-course servings

Red potatoes	1	**pound**
		(4 medium)
Yellow onion	1	**medium**
Olive oil	1	**tablespoon**
Marsala	2	**tablespoons**
Garlic	3	**cloves, minced**
Fresh rosemary leaves,		
minced	1	**tablespoon**
Whole eggs	2	**large**
Egg whites	4	**large**
Salt	¼	**teaspoon**
Pepper		**Several grinds**
Fresh pear tomatoes	⅓	**pound**
		(2 medium)
Balsamic vinegar	1	**tablespoon**

Scrub the potatoes but do not peel them; cut them into quarters or eighths, depending on their size. Place them in a
medium-size saucepan and cover with water. Put a lid on the
pan and bring to a boil over high heat. Remove the lid, reduce
heat to medium, and cook about 10 minutes, until potatoes are
barely fork-tender. Drain thoroughly and set aside.

Coarsely chop the onion. Heat the oil and Marsala in a
10-inch cast-iron skillet over medium heat. Stir in the onion,
garlic, and cooked potatoes, then add the rosemary. Sauté for
about 15 minutes, stirring frequently. The potatoes will become
lightly browned.

Meanwhile, crack the whole eggs into a large bowl and add the egg whites, salt, and pepper. Beat lightly with a whisk and set aside. Remove and discard the stem ends of the tomatoes, then cut them lengthwise into quarters. Preheat the broiler.

When the potatoes are tender all the way through, pour the egg mixture evenly into the skillet. Push the tomato wedges, skin side up, into the potato and egg mixture in a pretty pattern. Reduce the heat to low and cook, uncovered, for about 10 minutes, until all but the top is set. Place the skillet under the broiler and cook 2–3 minutes, until the top is set and the tomatoes are slightly charred. Remove from the oven and drizzle with the vinegar. Allow to sit for at least 10 minutes before serving. Serve from the pan, hot or at room temperature.

Each serving provides:

155	Calories	22 g	Carbohydrate
7 g	Protein	153 mg	Sodium
4 g	Fat	70 mg	Cholesterol
4 g	Dietary Fiber		

Index

Index

Index   *331*

Index　　　　　　　　　　　　　　　　　335

More **The Best 125** Cookbooks
by Mindy Toomay and Susann Geiskopf-Hadler

The Best 125 Meatless Pasta Dishes $16.00
Drawing on the cuisines of many nations, as well as the authors'
seasoned imaginations, this book expands your sense of pasta's
possibilities. With its emphasis on fresh ingredients and tantalizing flavors, this book proves we can eat less meat without sac-
rificing enjoyment. Recipes include Dried-Tomato Pesto with
Mint, Savory Pumpkin and Pasta Soup, Spinach Lasagna with
Port, and Tortellini Salad with Roasted Walnuts.

The Best 125 Meatless Main Dishes $14.95
Toomay and Geiskopf-Hadler once again team up to bring you
another collection of tantalizing and healthful meatless meals.
Their inventive dishes include Asparagus, Chevre, and Fresh
Dill Baked in Filo Pastry; Risotto with Porcini, Fresh Basil, and
Pine Nuts; Roasted Garlic, Red Pepper, and Ricotta Calzone
with Fresh Basil; and much more!

To Order Books

Please send me the following items:

Quantity	Title	Unit Price	Total
_____	_____	$ _____	$ _____
_____	_____	$ _____	$ _____
_____	_____	$ _____	$ _____
_____	_____	$ _____	$ _____
_____	_____	$ _____	$ _____

Shipping and Handling depend on Subtotal.

Subtotal	Shipping/Handling
$0.00–$14.99	$3.00
$15.00–$29.99	$4.00
$30.00–$49.99	$6.00
$50.00–$99.99	$10.00
$100.00–$199.99	$13.50
$200.00+	Call for Quote

Foreign and all Priority Request orders:
Call Order Entry department
for price quote at 916/632-4400

This chart represents the total retail price of books only
(before applicable discounts are taken).

Subtotal **$** _____

Deduct 10% when ordering 3-5 books **$** _____

7.25% Sales Tax (CA only) **$** _____

8.25% Sales Tax (TN only) **$** _____

5.0% Sales Tax (MD and IN only) **$** _____

Shipping and Handling* **$** _____

Total Order **$** _____

By Telephone: With MC or Visa, call 800-632-8676, 916-632-4400. Mon-Fri, 8:30-4:30.
WWW {http://www.primapublishing.com}

Orders Placed Via Internet E-mail {sales@primapub.com}

By Mail: Just fill out the information below and send with your remittance to:

Prima Publishing
P.O. Box 1260BK
Rocklin, CA 95677

My name is _____

I live at _____

City _____ State _____ Zip _____

MC/Visa# _____ Exp. _____

Check/Money Order enclosed for $ _____ Payable to Prima Publishing

Daytime Telephone _____

Signature _____